SURVIVAL TACTICS

PETER VANSITTART

SURVIVAL TACTICS
A LITERARY LIFE

8/46 12 45

PETER OWEN
London and Chester Springs

PETER OWEN PUBLISHERS
73 Kenway Road, London SW5 ORE

Peter Owen books are distributed in the USA by
Dufour Editions Inc., Chester Springs, PA 19425-0007

First published in Great Britain 1999
© Peter Vansittart 1999

ISBN 0 7206 1072 9

A catalogue record for this book is available from the British Library

Printed and bound in Great Britain by Hillman Printers (Frome) Ltd

To the Memory of Margot Walmsley
(1914–1997)

CONTENTS

1 Youth   9

2 Distant Planets   45

3 Detective Story   59

4 Novel Writing   69

5 Personalities   97

6 Growing Up   125

7 Movements   143

8 Conclusions   173

1

YOUTH

There move the enormous comics, drawn from life.

– W.H. Auden

For myself, that is all a writer is – a man working on the other side of a frontier.

– V.S. Pritchett

At the time of my birth in 1920, Lloyd George was Prime Minister. Monarchical Europe had largely vanished, its crowns scattered amongst the debris of the First World War, though Balkan courts remained lively sources of scandal. Elderly Frenchmen could still remember Napoleon III's disaster at Sedan and the atrocities of the Paris Commune and of its aftermath.

I remember the 1926 General Strike: angry crowds jostling outside Portsmouth Guildhall, adults oddly tense, the kitchen silent, my afternoon walk cancelled, the familiar turning strange. The postman, usually so friendly, now out of uniform, stood idle on a street corner, allowing our greeting only with a frozen stare. From the beggars and unemployed I had seen, there already hovered, behind regular meals and bedtime routines, a sense that the everyday was provisional, that I myself was on probation. I overheard rumours of naval mutiny at Gosport – 'rough as a bear and drunken as a Gosport Fiddler' wrote the future Poet Laureate John

Masefield, whose First World War letters I was to edit sixty years later.

Meanwhile, the adults continued to provide. Starvation – like massacre, sieges, charges – was stacked away in history, and in lurid tales of the First World War. I could not foresee that in my lifetime, for the first time since the Thirty Years War, cannibalism was to reappear in Europe: during Stalin's 'agrarian reform' – mass murder of peasants; during the siege of Leningrad; in the Nazi death camps, and in the disintegration of the Third Reich, when Koestler reported children killed and sold as veal on the black market. In China there was Mao's 'Great Leap Forward', in which 30 millions perished from starvation, parents eating their dead children, roadside corpses frantically devoured, through dogmatic and amateurish policies in agriculture, industry, one-party government.

I early felt some mystery, even romance, about myself, which separated me from the Michaels, Kits and Floras – at first because I was forbidden to row, dive from heights, climb steep hills and, inexplicably, train sheep-dogs, none of which distressed me but in fact enhanced my conviction of singularity. To this day I am liable unexpectedly to faint, often on occasions hideously or comically inappropriate, for reasons I have never nerved myself to discover. This has safeguarded me from the extremes of a terrible century. Save for some service during the London Blitz – 'Don't tell Mum,' a child whispered, dying, having ventured the streets, against orders – I have never been in real danger, fearing to be shoved against a wall and shot, sent to die in an Arctic or Polish camp for my beliefs, or lack of them, or threatened by a lynch mob.

I was told, told too often, that I was of a very old family – forbidding information that seemed to imply imminent extinction. My immediate family, however, was largely a gap in nature. My father had died before I was born; my mother, who soon remarried, never mentioned him, and I never asked. The new marriage transferred her to long periods abroad, which for me meant abrupt and frequent sojourns with various foster-parents, occasionally descending with a thud to a Children's Home. The last may well have impaired my self-confidence: years afterward, I heard some family friend mention 'that terrible frown', apparently characteristic of me at this period.

My mother had trained as a pianist in pre-1914 Germany. She had refused a proposal of marriage from the great pianist Solomon (to my relief he always ignored me) and claimed friendship with the French Empress Eugénie, sometimes recollecting that she had rested me on her knee. I could never substantiate this, but I did feel entitled to further promotion through this shadowy lady, whose husband, Napoleon III, had known Napoleon I, while she herself survived to befriend Jean Cocteau.

As for my father, his death certificate gave 'Occupation – Gentleman', and I know no more. I tended to invent heroic deaths for him: leading a charge at Mons, sinking on the bridge at Jutland, swooping on wings over Verdun. In romantic mood I would refer to myself as an orphan – once unwisely within earshot of my mother.

Subsequent investigations suggested my descent from a Netherlandish merchant, who was involved in some litigation in the Dukedom of Limburg in 1248. The family, mercantile, clerical, with sprigs of minor nobility, owed feudal allegiance to the Dukes of Limburg and Brabant – a flavour, I like to think, of Proust modified by Offenbach. When very young, I imagined I had thus been assigned a role, if not of absolute power, at least of consequence.

Sittart is a town near the Dutch–German border, where a medieval abbot from Outkamp built himself a private dwelling. In 1300 a certain Peter Vansittart owned a Cologne iron foundry. Following the Reformation, many descendants became Protestants, attracting some unpopularity in this Catholic city, so that a sixteenth-century John Vansittart emigrated to Danzig. The English clan originated with another Peter, born in 1670, a Baltic merchant. He refused offers from a Swedish Far Eastern trading house but became a director of the English East India Company from 1700, amassed wealth – none of it reaching myself – and bought a large mansion in the City of London (family plaques survive in the church of St Mary Axe). Some of my lifelong hankering for northern ports, solitary inlets, glittering Lapland nights, remote fishing villages, forests lit by the midnight sun and the Northern Lights, might thus come from a genetic inheritance.

There were other forebears. Dr Robert Vansittart was 'eminent for learning and worth and much esteemed by Dr Johnson'. Johnson once suggested they climb a wall, but Robert demurred. The family home was Bisham Abbey, Berkshire, where the more riotous members sought the antics of the Hell Fire Club at West Wycombe. Nicholas Vansittart, Lord Bexley, Chancellor of the Exchequer, introduced Income Tax as a temporary expedient during the Napoleonic wars. Brigadier General Vansittart was assessed in Martinique, 1801, as 'gentlemanlike but from want of habit not to have the tone or manner of command', while Admiral Edward Vansittart 'suppressed piracy in China, 1852–5' (*DNB*). Such activities played an unexceptional part in the history of the times. But I now reflect that, if sometimes brutally extortionate, the British Empire perhaps did more good than harm in Asia and Africa and compares well enough to the societies admired by its fiercest critics. This, even after Dennis Potter's laugh about 'the hideous residue of the White Man's Burden' having been cleared out of the reading rooms of schoolboys, I have maintained, and it betrays my age and my mildly affectionate feelings for Britain; though in 1997 some 900 primary school children were interviewed: only one-third were proud of being English, for such reasons as 'because Manchester United is English or 'We won the World Cup in 1966'. Historical figures were not mentioned.

T.E. Lawrence, 'Prince of Mecca', was a distant relation, grandson of William Chapman, descendant of a cousin of Sir Walter Raleigh and who married Martha Louisa Vansittart. Among my more contemporary relatives was Robert Gilbert Vansittart, Permanent Under-Secretary for Foreign Affairs (1930–8) and Chief Diplomatic Adviser to the Government (1938–41). He was also minor poet, novelist and dramatist, whose *Dead Heat* shared the bill with George Bernard Shaw at a Malvern Festival. He also wrote movie scripts for his neighbour, Alexander Korda, contributing to the exotic 1940 film *The Thief of Baghdad*.

Resolutely pro-French and anti-German, in the thirties he was anxious to detach Mussolini from German temptations and drafted preliminaries to the reviled pact with France to connive at the conquest of Ethiopia. His anti-appeasement stance elicited scant sympathy from Prime Minister Neville Chamberlain, though the historian A.J.P. Taylor asserted that this was due less to his advice than to the Proustian intricacies of his memoranda. In 1940, with France tottering, he and the Foreign Secretary, Lord Halifax, drew up for Churchill, in collusion with de Gaulle and Monnet, a Declaration of Indissoluble Anglo-French Union. This, however, was swiftly negated by German capture of Paris. 'They want to make us another Dominion,' Pétain protested.

This background made me feel stationed in history (if without, in my early years, much personal effort). My mother, meanwhile, on her periodic reappearances, would take me to visit affluent friends with country houses and at least one castle, Bletsoe, whose very rich owners she had, sensibly but ultimately uselessly, selected as my godparents. Of Bletsoe I remember only a cobbled yard, a water-butt and Terence, a stable-boy about whom I concocted tales of being born of a giant and a wild boar. He always addressed me as 'matey', with which I began to greet other castle guests until discouraged by brisk ill will.

These changes of locale and acquaintance constantly encouraged me to alter my demeanour, responses, loyalties. To me, fairy stories made obvious sense, based as they were on transformation, riddles, tests, the workings of fate.

I have been assured that the self, ego, personality, even identity, are fluid. I have not found it so. Perhaps to my discredit, I remain scared, amused, intrigued by the same things that affected me in Bletsoe days; constantly attracted to and fooled by similar physical and intellectual types. Similarly, my love for *The Snow Queen*, *Little Women*, *The Three Hostages* and the richly bound *Asgard and the Gods* remains undaunted.

This conviction of psychic stability was to crystallize in my 1960 novel *A Sort of Forgetting*. In a Nazi death camp, prisoners are ordered to build a gallows. A Polish Jew – veteran, master carpenter, impatient at their inexpertise – volunteers to supervise. Even in this charnel house, with life ground to a few twitching shreds, he retains endemic pride, thumbing the wood, inspecting the tools, calculating tensions and balance. His eye, his spirit, revive; he gives orders, finds each prisoner a task. The others slump, as they realize they are constructing their own death. Yet the old man will not be denied; exactitude of hand and eye, blade and chisel is vital, and some, galvanized, promise him their best.

Such behaviour, of course, is not altogether admirable. It can symbolize stagnation or defeatism; also some essential human trait, some hankering for order, symmetry, even perfection.

Already by the age of seven I had learnt that life was provisional, other people were unpredictable, and attention to myself was perfunctory. It was best to rely on nobody. I was retreating deep into imagination, disliking most other children almost as much as I did adults. Adults created quarrels, they shouted, they caused wars, they hurried to the Bank and returned slowly. Fathers wanted huge Daimlers, mothers demanded more money. Perched on the sidelines, I dreaded being asked when I was going to school; also, being ordered to dance, to assist the conjurer, eat boiled mutton, sing a solo.

I cherish the day when I first found myself, not loudly spelling out words but reading silently. The gate in the wall had opened, slants of light revealed limitless enchantments. I sought stories, caring nothing for distinctions between truth and fiction, but read whatever was to hand, much of it unthinkable for today's children. With some misgiving I pored over Charles Wesley's 'A Mother's Thanksgiving for the Death of her Child':

> There is an hour when I must die,
> Nor do I know how soon 'twill come.
> A thousand children young as I
> are called by Death to meet their doom.

Meanwhile, Isaac Watts' hymn outlined divine wrath at youthful disobedience:

> The ravens shall pick out his eyes
> And eagles eat the same.

I imagined God as a tall electric light bulb, unaware that such light depended upon human co-operation but dimly realizing that it did not distinguish between the good and the bad. Instructed that God damned disrespect for parents – itself easy to display – I did not know of Pavlick

Morozov, a Soviet boy martyr venerated for denouncing his parents for 'anti-state activities', assisting kulaks in 1932. He himself was later murdered.

Unconcerned with the habits of the stickleback or the meaning of 'monastic', I chanted mysterious lines from a Norse saga:

> Swift in counsel, Bifrost's
> Guardian struggles with the
> Son of Laufey, wondrous, subtle,
> At Singastein, avid for the necklace.

I had an eye for familiar words planted in unexpected places: a Nigerian story began: 'Udo Ubock Udom was a famous king who lived at Ham, which is an island town, and does not possess a river. The King and his wife therefore used to wash at the spring just behind their house.' Today, when bored, I irritate others by muttering 'Udo Ubock Udom'.

In a recurrent dream, usually after prolonged illicit reading, I found myself falling through a pit past protruding tusked and maned heads, then somehow bounced back amongst pallid tombstones. I was not then tormented by any idea that such dreams could be explained, whether by fear of sexuality, obsession with South Africa or memory of a grandmother chased by a rat during the Prussian siege of Paris.

In another dream, through many years, I watched a house – long, low, white, pillared, with blue shutters – standing in a woodland clearing, surrounded by walled gardens, tennis lawns, statues, very distinct in hard, clear, northern light. People stood about, women in long dresses, men in riding clothes, talking intensely. Always a girl ran past, in green coat and skirt, soundless, ignored, soon vanishing. Today, I am at last writing a novel, set in Estonia, exploring that house, its inhabitant, the story of the girl, whom villagers said at last ran over a cliff, the edge of the world.

From maids – as unthinkable in my present home as a platypus – I gathered rumours and gossip. Even now I half-believe in the murderer down the road, perhaps the 'Captain Ferguson' in Auden's poem 'Taller

To-Day'. Once a maid unexpectedly thrust at my penis and whispered, 'Do you know that this is for?' It had not occurred to me that I did not. An incident, I realize, almost obligatory for the period.

Maids, newspaper headlines, adults' half-understood exchanges, gave me sensations of lurking behind the scenes in some drama – nameless, fragmented but insistent – which I have never lost, protecting me from boredom, mindless ogres and the abyss. I have been cosseted not by routine but by intimations, however unreal, of the hidden side of things.

The more I see of friends, the less I seem to know them, an ignorance confirmed by their obituaries. We exchange the clichés not of intimacy but of regular social contact. The glance, intonation, smile of a stranger instantly revives the feelings of queer secrets or glamour reserved for myself alone. This reminds me of a suggestion in Broch's *The Death of Virgil* that the smile, essence of human compatibility, is where language began.

To present-day youth I must seem to have survived from an archaic and disreputable age, when, for example, family prayers were a feature of everyday life. The domestic employees stood, starched, capped, aproned, in blacks and whites, or in brown livery, as if posed for a photograph. Seldom present was the gardener, Mr Friend, who lived to be a hundred but by some irregularity failed to receive the royal telegram, so that I wondered later whether he had been confused with the movie-maker, George Pal. Meanwhile, the maids grinned maliciously at his stooping back and giggled that he wouldn't make old bones, though I wondered why he should wish to. For prayers, the family was seated, rigid, as though at a concert. But beyond them, beyond neat lawns and select arbours, were realms, dangerous but alluring, waiting to be charted: jungaloid acres, locked sheds in woods, walls too high to climb, concealing the forbidden; and attics crammed with the lost and extraordinary. These always remained: in Tripoli where walled gardens reached through orange groves to the sea, enclosing absolute stillness and who knows what; in a courtyard at Poznan where human shadows continually criss-crossed on thin curtains; in an unnaturally silent cul-de-sac in Kilburn where, at sixty, I whispered, 'The Valley of Fear'.

So much seemed to wish to bow acquaintance, make demands. A tree, a bird, a lamp-lighter transforming the air, a muttering, gristle-faced tramp, all seemed to say, 'Tell our stories.' On one tree a dog had been hanged; the heavy war-memorial pressed down the ghosts of grenadiers; in certain lights a bush was transformed to white gloves hanging on different levels. For each toy soldier I invented names, for infamy, for wonder. This one had betrayed Monmouth or the Prince Imperial, that one had brought good news through a whirl of bullets. Two had marched to Kandahar with secret messages, another had that mysterious 'touch of the tar brush' so deplored by pearled ladies with sharp voices.

Stories lay around me: once I saw a footprint on the ceiling, a permanent image of the inexplicable, perhaps of watchful eyes on the other side of the air. Ceilings, furniture, shadows, people, quivered on the edge of multiple transformations, striving to emerge, crystallizing in my 1958 novel *The Tournament*, set in fifteenth-century Burgundy.

This room was called *Forest* because of the picture drawn in lost Tartar inks. In early morning you saw a wood, dark leaves arrested like frozen tears and, beneath, a tall woodcutter, a girl with a doll, birds on a branch above a pool. Later, as the light turned, the wood became blurred and swollen; only the woodcutter remaining distinct. The girl and birds had vanished. Young and strong, the woodcutter stood entire, his axe shrunk, new inks were exposed making the pool a rushing river, the birds one bird, shrill and unappeasable. The child had returned, kneeling in fear, the doll lost. The forest had deepened in hush. By dangerous twilight there were only huge, separate shadows, but, when sconces were lit, the whole reappeared: the woodman was standing in calm, secure light with the girl, the doll, the birds and the protecting trees.

Hating to talk, I kept stories and discoveries very private, and even today I shrink from conversation, save gossip, or about sport, movies and the novels of Patrick White.

For some years I was a guest at an annual Christmas Eve dinner, together with John Bayley and Iris Murdoch. Even for me, Professor Bayley was easy, ebullient, his chuckles and constant agreements demolishing my reserve. Iris Murdoch, whom I much admired, though smiling, was cryptic, courteously aloof, so that, when forced to address her, anxious as I was to know her opinions of current literature, art, politics – alas, I could only nervously stammer out whatever *non sequitur* floated into my head. I was like a young performer in a Shakespeare play. My self-disgust was partly modified when, meeting another formidably gifted Oxonian lady, I remarked that life in Oxford must be stimulating with such people as Iris Murdoch around. She gazed at me in wonder. 'Iris Murdoch. I've seen her several times a week for eleven years and all she ever says to me is "Hallo, old thing! How goes it!"' Never mind. More important, I could learn from Iris Murdoch's books, notably: 'The practice of any art is a moral discipline, a struggle against fantasy, against self-indulgence.'

At seven, I was convinced that monkeys, dogs, butterflies, even slugs, had once been human, but, through accident, illness or misbehaviour, had degenerated – although dragons, flying geese, an occasional horse, suggested that improvement on humans was possible. My beliefs were confirmed on Dartmoor by a knowing adult, who pointed to a black pig and said it was the spirit of Judge Jeffreys. Only the other day I learnt that Canadian Hurons believed that beavers had once enjoyed human-like intelligence and speech but had been demoted by the Great Spirit for presumption.

By making imagination more restricted, providing models on which to test my perceptions, books tempted me to discard primal innocence, though I never wholly succumbed. Classical myths – girls becoming reeds or swallows, iron filings transformed to warriors, gods to bulls and rainbows – made me watch for centaurs and wonder if they were superior or inferior to ourselves. Certainly, they were not, in a then over-used phrase, 'People like us'.

In verses by Kipling and de la Mare I found further metamorphoses, sometimes of uncanny magic, which I could later understand as metaphor, vital addition to consciousness. I still relish, even depend upon, the oblique, mysterious, half-seen, the barely understood or even the misunderstood. My imagination was excited by the phrase 'Shooting the Rapids', implying its ill-natured whites potting at Indian braves who indeed departed very rapidly. I recall too, that, when young, Freud's biographer Ernest Jones saw an adult point across a Welsh bay and mis-heard 'That's Devon'; thereafter he believed that *Heaven* was visible on clear days.

Already I thought myself not better than other boys, probably worse, but possessing a knowledge that was nagging, sometimes painful, but very, very important. I had seen death in a Devonshire lane: a shadow stumbled from a dripping hedge, hardened into a gaunt, feverish cripple, who stretched imploring hands at a stationary car which at once sped away, leaving me in sudden chill, as if kissed by Mr Dombey.

Nomadic shuffles between foster-homes, each in a different way absorbing and odd, helped insure me against what R.D. Laing was to term primary ontological insecurity. I later survived a brief but pleasant acquaintance with Laing, who was always, I supposed, at his best – humorous, inquisitive, friendly – though I never risked telling him that I suffered no problems of self-identity or split personality, while fre-quently objecting to the slight, only too readily definable personality I did possess. My insecurity derived from convictions that I was awkward and ugly and would win no prizes. Magic mirrors whispered 'Others are Better.' Adults, however, changed their personality as frequently as the weather, suggesting that each thought of himself, herself, not as *I* but as *We*, a multitude of selves.

Wherever I lived, books were waiting to be read, indiscriminately. Adults were too busy to censor my discoveries. That I often understood very little was no impediment, rather, a stimulant, vital as some Tudor seaman pointing westward. Today I rage against those who purge and simplify children's books, in the interests of class, race, gender and belief that readers lack imagination and intelligence. A school edition of *King Solomon's Mines* shorn of words over two syllables, references to blacks, titles of nobility, and reduced to 120 pages, mocks belief in progress. I am moved to purring nostalgia by memory of musty old books once read deep into the night in unfamiliar bedrooms, in tents on rainy afternoons, in an Express Dairy café, on Hampstead Heath. My own two books on the French Revolution had roots in *The Scarlet Pimpernel* and its creator, Baroness Orczy, inspired by the sight of a stranger standing alone in the Temple underground station. I wondered whether Orczy was a high-born Hungarian bandit or whether 'Baroness' was her Christian name, perhaps self-awarded. Quite recently, I read that she had founded an Active Service League, women handing out white feathers to men who had not enlisted during the First World War. She would have been stalled by the tub-shaped G.K. Chesterton; when some harpy hissed 'Why aren't you out at the Front?', he patted his stomach. 'Madam, I *am* out at the Front.'

I would toy with words, have done not much more ever since. I loved to murmur *Summer House,* emblem of harmony, refuge, the timelessness of a child's afternoon, afterwards a setting for a Henry James heroine, Saki's dandies and minor conspiracies. I knew many summer houses: miniature pagodas, tiny Italianate villas, scaled-down salons. One stood on a turntable, revolving with the sun, like a mystical glass tower in Celtic myth.

In an essay on his early reading, *The Lost Childhood*, Graham Greene cited the opening of A.E.W. Mason's *The Watchers*, which for me conveys more poetry than much of *The Oxford Book of Twentieth-Century English Verse*.

> It was the story of a youth that sat in the stocks of a Sunday morning and disappeared from the islands; of a girl named Helen; of a negro who slept; and of men watching a house with a great tangled garden that stood at the edge of the sea.

In old age, I was allowed the privilege of repaying a debt to two authors I think of as my real godfathers, by introducing *These for Remembrance* in 1987, a hitherto unpublished book by John Buchan, and editing a new edition of H.G. Wells' *Kipps* published in 1993.

Back in 1928 I inhabited a perimeter of picturesque nonsense:

> Mr East gave a feast,
> Mr North laid the cloth,
> Mr West did his best,
> Mr South burnt his mouth
> 　　　　eating cold pease pudding.

Further insets revive from *long ago*. Silent films showing Douglas Fairbanks in endless pirouettes – dodging, leaping, plunging in dizzy swirls and feints like a many-armed god. He escaped from dungeons, curvetted from roof to roof, achieved the grand impossible, suggesting the infinite resources of body, imagination, will.

Once I saw George V, bearded, solemn, small, descending steps. It sounds trivial but was not. The steps were numerous and steep, but, while his uniformed retinue moved cautiously and clumsily, the King moved, without once looking down, in a smooth, continuous, rhythmical line, unhurried and inevitable as falling water, giving me an instance of perfection.

George V's wife, Queen Mary, was stately, toqued, descended from Genghis Khan, though, despite her reputed addiction to kleptomania, without much moral or physical resemblance. Once, teaching in Rhyl, I demonstrated how easily history can be forged, mythologized, manipulated. I told my pupils, very loudly, in a public place, that Queen Mary had a wooden leg. Two days later, in a cinema when Queen Mary appeared on a newsreel, a nearby woman whispered, 'Did you know . . . wooden leg?'

From 1928 to 1938, at boarding school, I was engrossed with sport, books, a desire to be popular as the Prince of Wales, amusing as Noël Coward, to be in the swim yet, simultaneously, out of it.

From a chaplain I learnt that 'Pharisee' means 'separated'. With my private convictions and mental pictures I felt I was an unmistakable Pharisee, not a wholly enviable role, since it carried the imputation that I was hated by Jesus. As late as 1986, a fellow pupil whom I had not seen since 1933, having read something I had published, wrote to me: 'I remember you. You were like me, an oaf, sullen, one of the herd.' My conviction of ambiguous isolation had been reinforced by early discovering that I was the only circumcised boy in the dormitory. What did this denote? Disease, said a wiseacre, probably fatal. Others' curiosity I mistook for fear, suspicion, ridicule. 'Why,' my mother would reiterate – like thousands of mothers throughout the land – 'can't you be like other boys?' I wanted it too, yet there were few I envied or admired – very few,

21

I thought, who treasured *Summer House* or *The Rapids*. Wanting exorbitant love, I was yet proud of walking alone.

Once, exploring my mother's handbag in search of coins for a Nat Gonella record, I found a part of a letter from my headmaster. The page ended: 'Peter's smile will win him many friends, but . . .' The rest was missing and I have often wondered how he completed it.

I watched people for signs of friendship, even intimacy, but guardedly. I have never wholly believed that others' addresses and telephone numbers are not tricks to deceive the inquisitive and unwanted. I am quietly surprised if letters reach their destination or a familiar voice answers my call. Perhaps related to all this is my dislike of addressing anyone by name, though it may also have affinity with the primitive belief that uttering a name has, like certain numbers and colours, a fateful, even dangerous, significance.

Much in my prep school became material for novel-writing. On Friday nights, for example, coconut oil was rubbed painfully into our heads, a ritual someone interpreted as the authorities' design to make us as docile as trees. My novels are saturated with such memories, recollections of the 'enormous comics', comedians who turned terrible, buffoons in absolute power, favourites weeping after their fall, lunatics hailed as messiahs; embryo crooks, medicine-men, heroes, sad-eyed actors, and indeed authors.

My school life had an unwholesome beginning, which was to find its way into the writing of *A Sort of Forgetting* in 1960. The school had gone to the local swimming baths. One boy, a licensed clown and teacher's favourite, dived from an aching height in a graceful curve but did not reappear. Some of us could see him, far below, outspread, writhing in hazed dance. The master bawled at him to stop showing off and trying to be funny, the rest of us joining in, 'Stop showing off' to the rhythm of a hymn. By some fluke, he had caught his thumb in an underwater grating and, funny no longer, drowned under a network of jubilant eyes.

With such promptings already stored, I had already by the age of nine begun to write, preparing a mammoth history of England with all dates, battles and women omitted – not by design but from the lack of information to hand. Like many others, I imagine, I made no conscious

decision to write, merely following my pen into exotic territories while some tired voice explained the advantages of the subjunctive, the deficiencies of Ahab or how the Romans said 'yes'. Much continues to surprise me. To one master I owed a great deal, in his reading aloud from Wells, Saki, Kipling, for his constant loan of books – Homer, Conrad, Bennett – for tireless encouragement for me to read further. He died in his seventies, and his widow told me that, after being forbidden further golf, he had died of boredom.

'But, surely, Grace – his love of books . . .'

'No. Graham hated reading. He once remarked about Arnold Bennett that the kindest thing to say was that he was completely worthless.'

From such men and women I subsequently learnt of Pound and Eliot; Auden and Graves; Michelet, Tawney, Eileen Power; Marx and his Theory of Surplus Value. I was to be delighted to hear of James Joyce telling Herbert Gorman that he had read nothing of Marx save the first sentence of *Capital*, which he found so absurd that he could not continue. Harold Wilson apparently began the book, discovered on page three a footnote longer than the page's text and desisted.

Masters also had reserves of high comedy and low farce. On Ascension Day the Headmaster arose in his grandeur: 'For this commemoration of an event so important to human well-being, I am granting a whole holiday.' A junior master stood up to congratulate the speaker in this responsible, if belated, acknowledgement of the resignation of the Foreign Secretary, Sir Samuel Hoare.

In my teens I was surrounded by those who were seemingly assured and fluent, charming but suspect, ludicrous yet vicious, but most were impenetrable. I admired, imitated or despised them, wanted to be invited by intimate coteries, but they passed me as if blind. I was left with but one certainty, a shred of moral achievement – the resolution to write their stories, expose their nobility or vileness, forcing them at last to acknowledge their large, ugly contemporary who was useful at cricket but not much else. Periodically, in novels, I have done so, though the characters take wing, flee far from their originals, showing me that I had known them even less than I had supposed.

The Second World War upset many of my provisional assessments of people. There was Selwyn 'Pip' Fraser-Smith, whom I saw daily for four years: blue-eyed, flaxen-haired, almost embarrassingly unexceptional, he seemed destined to vanish into a bank, civil service or family firm. School finished, we never met again: I had his address but never used it, there was always plenty of time. I occasionally thought of him, without obvious reason: while buying a carpet in Damascus, in the Pushkin Gallery, Moscow, and once, in Virginia, I thought I saw him in a passing car.

But there is never plenty of time. Reading his *Times* obituary in 1996, I realized yet again my own imperceptions, and the opaqueness of others. During the war, it transpired, Pip had served with V Force, an intelligence unit working behind Japanese lines in Burma.

> Fraser-Smith's courage and endurance astonished his comrades. One day he swam the Chindwin river – about a quarter of a mile wide at that point – in broad daylight under the noses of the Japanese in order to steal a boat and rescue two men. On another occasion, after crossing a river at night, he crept into a hut where three Japanese officers were sleeping and removed vital documents. Though much taller, at six feet two, than the average Japanese, Fraser-Smith succeeded in moving among their forward troops even when they were deployed for attack, and his reports from the front were models of clarity and of great value to the British. Frequently stricken by malaria, jungle sores and the pains of a camp virtually waterless and reached only by a 3,000 feet climb, Pip refused all leave until, injuring himself at football with Gurkhas, he was forcibly repatriated.

Reading this, I suddenly realized that several of my fictional characters partly derived from a subconscious awareness of his essence, together with that of Ian Souter and Alan Ross.

Alan, who today is known as a poet, autobiographer, travel writer and editor of *London Magazine*, I knew at school only as cricketer with a fine, high-stepping bowling action, wearing clothes superior to the general cut and a manner and speech that were charming, lightly hesitant, but with a hint of the supercilious. To me, whilst I was peacocking in college magazines, he never once mentioned books, and I had no notion that a master – whom I had seen only as very worthy and dull, though Wilfrid Blunt told me in 1990 that he paid a young ostler to visit him twice a week – was introducing Alan to the poetry of De Vigny, Lamartine, Verlaine.

I had no instinct for discovering the reserves that sustained Alan through the mortal dangers of serving in ships taking arms to Murmansk. In one action his destroyer engaged German cruisers and a pocket battleship; his captain won the VC, in this combat, which had crucial effects on the naval campaign. Once Alan was left on a sinking ship with fire blazing above the magazine. 'We'll try and get someone to relieve you when we can,' the First Lieutenant said, rather unconvincingly, 'but for the moment, I'm afraid you're on your own.' Such activities produced from Alan some of the most substantial naval poetry of the war: as an evocation of his own sensitivities under stress but also as a narrative of wartime service. In post-war Germany he played bridge with Ronald Chesney – naval officer, psychopath, drug racketeer, gambler, suspected murderer – and narrowly escaped being pushed into providing an alibi for a proposed killing. Once, in a cricket match, he was batting when a fielder set his pubic hair ablaze through unwisely secreting a box of matches in his trouser pocket.

I myself may survive only in a verse of Alan's poem 'Arena at Arles'.

> The voice returns, droning *Next, next, translate*
> *A passage, Vansittart, Ross*, politely, *Would it bore you?*
> While all the time summer was cramming our nostrils –
> Cut-grass, roses, a cricket match going on
> Somewhere, far away as our minds
> Never much occupied with Daudet and his mill,
> But rehearsing desire, scribbling the blank horizon.

Seldom seeing people whole, I have been fascinated by Marxist agents who, while outwardly scrupulous public figures, secretly communicate in codes, betray secrets, send fellow countrymen to the bullet or rope. A friend's personalities would have to be hung like signal flags, varied for marriage and love-affairs, office, home and pub: for myself, for others. At my tennis club I often believe that all members save myself exist only as players, so that, on leaving the premises, they actually die, returning as ghosts, reviving only on court. It was a shock to realize that Barbara Mills, long familiar as a vigorous but not savage player, was also Director of Public Prosecutions; that Zander, gracious but taciturn, was elsewhere a fluent Professor of Medieval French Poetry. Kenneth Lo admitted to several identities – diplomat, author, Davis Cup tennis player, restaurateur, master of Chinese cuisine. His tennis technique involved waving his racket many times before serving, inducing nervous strain and occasional heart failure in his opponent, thereby fulfilling a Taoist proverb that the sage accomplishes everything without doing it.

It is often assumed that boarding schools destroy individuality, sensitivity, the imagination and heterosexual responses. I did not find it so, though they told me much that I already knew: that self-reliance was more dependable than prayers, contracts, pledges; that experts are usually wrong and saints very suspect (Orwell remarked that it took a great deal of money to keep Gandhi in poverty). I had early known the truth of a verse I heard during the fifties:

> The rain it raineth every day
> upon the just and unjust fella,
> But more upon the just, because
> the unjust steals the just's umbrella.

I have learnt to expect nothing, thereby profiting by usually gaining a little. I always had expectations not of plenty but of scarcity, even famine, and early fortified myself against disappointment, beginning with an 'aunt's' promise to give me 'paper' for my birthday. I envisaged a glistening, crackling £5 note but received instead a copy of Arthur Mee's *The Children's Newspaper*, instructive, moral and unreadable. A similar rebuff occurred after my wedding. Strategically, I took my wife to visit a distant relative – very distant, very rich. We were welcomed, given a generous tea, and we exchanged gratified smiles which redoubled when the relative, visibly in terminal decline, quavered, 'Now, my dears, I hope you will not object, but I'm giving you your wedding present in an envelope.'

We affected unconcern, my wife's habitual expression of quiet purity was useful, but once outside we rushed behind the nearest tree agog for the riches of the Indies. The envelope contained a pamphlet on the virtues and duties of marriage, privately printed at considerable expense.

Corporal punishment? Ah, yes. I was twice beaten: once by an anaemic, non-playing prefect for helping lose a match in which I scored three tries and a dropped goal; and once when a question was asked during a scripture lesson. The correct answer was 'Jesus', which I supplied, but the master misheard this for 'Jeeves' and reported me for irreverence.

Such matters did not, I think, irreparably damage my psyche, but were useful demonstrations that authority is often ludicrous, its aims obscure, its exponents pitiable. When Churchill was beaten at Harrow, he cheerfully told the prefect, 'I'll be a greater man than you'.

Books remained my impregnable stronghold. To adapt a line of Ezra Pound's, much reading was as good as having a home. Though lacking Sexton Blake and Bulldog Drummond, the college libraries were ample. I mulled over a battered Tennyson which, like Homer and the Sagas, enclosed me in the remote yet tangible, arousing a melancholy but indefinable nostalgia, perhaps aroused by memories real or imagined of heavy and dusty old rooms, early deaths, drowsy gardens shaded by ancient cypresses, an Arcadia of urns brimming with hyacinth and lily, adorned with fountains, draped with a vague sexuality.

> Dear Mother Ida, hearken ere I die . . .
> It was deep midnoon: one silvery cloud
> Had lost its way between the piney sides
> Of this long glen. Then to the bower they came,
> Naked they came to that smooth-swarded bower,
> And at their feet the crocus brake like fire . . .

Pushkin maintained that to read poetry in translation resembles

smelling flowers through a blanket. Nevertheless, I was haunted by
Helen Waddell's translation of a Chinese poem of 700 BC:

> The tribulus grew on the wall,
> > upon the stain.
> The things done in that inner room
> > men cannot name.
> The tribulus grows on the wall,
> > the stain is old,
> The evil of that inner room
> > may not be told.

I enjoyed reading about downfalls and recovery – Rome, France,
Germany – and relished the odd, rather than the fantastic. Attracted by
its title, I bought second-hand Jacob Wasserman's *The Triumph of Youth*
(1916), which fifty years later gave me some inklings for *A Safe Conduct.*
The same writer's *The Goose Man*, from 1915, held me by its portrait of
Herr Carovius, an avid newspaper reader:

Nothing escaped him, neither a murder in a Pomeranian village nor the
loss of a pearl necklace in the Boulevard des Italiens; neither the founder-
ing of a steamer in the South Seas, nor a fashionable wedding at
Westminster; neither the chit-chat about new fashions, nor a massacre of
the Armenians by the Turks; neither the obituary of a great magnate nor
the report of the arrest of a tramp. Joyful events like births, investitures,
the winning of a lottery first prize, the success of a new book or a lucky
speculation, had no effect on him, or perhaps even annoyed him. In contrast, his imagination grasped with delight at whatever he discovered
about the evil, sad, lamentable, on earth or in the universe.

Whenever he enlarged his experience by some event curious or
unprecedented, he took out his pocket book, made a note of the date, and
wrote: 'At Amberg a priest broke a blood-vessel while preaching a sermon.' 'In Cochin-China a tiger devoured thirteen children, leapt into a
settler's bungalow and bit off the head of a woman sleeping beside her
husband.' 'At Copenhagen, a woman of ninety, formerly an actress, stood

on a basket in the middle of the market-place and recited Lady Macbeth's monologue; this created such excitement that several people in the crowd were crushed to death.' He then went home very happy.

From Herr Carovius I learnt the importance of pocket-books, and I have used them since I was fifteen. I choose one page at random.

Around 155 AD, Ireland was briefly divided between Conn of the Hundred Battles (North) and Eoghan Mor, King of Munster (South).

Charles Ducaire, secretary to Cardinal-Archbishop Gerbier, sheltered Paul Touvier, collaborator with the Lyons Gestapo, in rounding up Jews for extermination.

In *Little Men*, by Louisa May Alcott (1868), to cure a boy of lying, Professor Bhaer, instead of punishing him, asked him to cane him instead.

John Wayne loathed horses.

Cuba, 1994, officially denounced suicide as 'a non-revolutionary position.

'Youth today is casual, ill-mannered, and disrespectful to older people.' – Socrates

'Nothing shocks me, but myself.' – General Charles Gordon

Islam maintains that nine species of animal can reach Paradise.

Robert Furlong, former Chief Justice of Newfoundland, died 1996, and had been engaged for 59 years until his fiancée's death.

'The Sultan Ibrahim, being of a particularly self-indulgent nature, once dispatched his whole Harem, 300 strong, for the pleasure of being able to restock it with refreshing newcomers. A diver off Seraglio Point came up with tales of dead bodies all standing upright, weighted by their feet, swaying and bowing in the underwater swell with a sort of ghastly politeness.' – Lesley Blanch, *The Wilder Shores of Love* (1954)

'I don't think Mr Greenwood would be fit for any duty, because he has been idle all his life, and is very fond of good living, but a deanery would just suit him.' – Anthony Trollope, *Marion Fay* (1881–2)

On the memorial to Sir Henry Pottinger, first Governor of Hong Kong is: 'On concluding his successful Treaty with China in the year

1842, he was Destined for the Peerage by Her Gracious Majesty Queen Victoria the First, but Lost this High Distinction through the same Hostile Influence which was exerted in vain to Prevent Parliament Rewarding his Excellent Services to the State.'

In Javanese, *Prostitute* and *Toy* are identical.

These notes are wholly unsystematic, resolutely uncomputerized, so that to check one small fact I may have to explore a dozen notebooks, thus giving myself a refresher course and turning up the diverting or useful. Similarly, Patrick Leigh Fermor, looking up the mating habits of crocodiles on the River Volta, found himself reading the complete works of Voltaire.

From school-days onwards, lazy about learning foreign languages, I have been dependent on translators. I have been grateful to Bede, King Alfred, Wycliffe, Tyndale, translators who enlarged the English mind, not forgetting John Hoole (1727–1803), translator of Tasso and Ariosto, of whom Walter Scott remarked that he was a noble transmuter of gold into lead. Sir Thomas Urquhart (1611–60), translator of Rabelais, appropriately died of laughter at Charles II's restoration.

Less cheerfully, I discovered an American Bible which rendered 'Whoever strikes another man and kills him shall be put to death' as 'Don't waste nobody. It ain't cool.'

I would like to read in the original, Pasternak's

> Life, like autumn silence,
> Is always deep in details.

As an adult I realized when in Russia that such words as *lawn*, *garden*, *sunflower*, *birch*, *pond* must convey to my hosts nuances very different from my own. Likewise, *safe*, *alone*, *protection* and names and colours with their religious, historical and familial associations and symbolism. Robert A. Maguire and John E. Malmstad, introducing their translation of Andrei Bely's *Petersburg* (1916), point out the intricacies of the apparently simple 'a yellow house'.

The institutions and private houses lining the English Embankment are painted with a pale yellow colour. Because state-owned buildings are often painted in that colour, *yellow house* became an euphemism for an insane asylum; in fact, for Russians, this is the primary meaning for the expression. Yellow is the dominant colour used in descriptions of Petersburg by many Russian writers, especially the symbolists, for whom the colour of this urban setting has a malevolent and sinister overtone.

Nabokov said that, for him, the twentieth century's prose masterpieces were, in order, Joyce's *Ulysses*, Kafka's *Metamorphosis*, Bely's *Petersburg* and the first half of Proust's 'fairy-tale'.

I have always relished Thomas Mann in Helen Lowe-Porter's translations and was depressed to read, in Ronald Hayman's 1995 biography of Mann, 'She often failed to notice the ironical undertones, and sometimes damaged the text by leaving out phrases when she failed to understand either their function or their meaning. In *Death in Venice* she omits the last sentence of the penultimate paragraph.'

At school, I read little foreign poetry but enjoyed novels and biographies by such writers as Stefan Zweig, Franz Werfel, Heinrich Mann, Alfred Neumann, Victor Hugo, Guy de Maupassant. In his study of Unity Mitford David Pryce-Jones mentions that no English youngster in the thirties read Lion Feuchtwanger's *Jew Süss* (published in 1925), but, for once, he was mistaken. It was available everywhere, assisted, no doubt, by the English movie version staring Conrad Veidt. Its beginning at once entranced me.

A network of roads, like veins, was strung over the land, interlacing, branching, dwindling to nothing. They were neglected, full of stones and holes, torn up, overgrown, bottomless swamps in wet weather, and, besides, everywhere impeded by toll gates. In the south, among the mountains, they narrowed into bridle-paths and disappeared. All the blood of the land flowed through these veins. The bumpy roads, gaping with dusty cracks in the sun, heavy with mud in the rain, were the moving life of the land, its breath and pulse.

I felt that I too was on those roads, jostling with the scrawny King of Prussia, the wily Prince-Archbishop of Salzburg, the florid, apoplectic Duke of Württemberg, along with seditious scholars and plump chamberlains. I listened to itinerant players and cattlemen, furred merchants, sweating monks, secretive couriers. I dodged the calèche of the Venetian ambassador – a figure omnipresent throughout western history – and the handcarts of Jewish pedlars. I joked with mountebanks – splendid word, almost forgotten today when, in the media, mountebanks are inescapable – and argued with pilgrims about the meaning of Resurrection. I was sold dud gold by alchemists, was incautiously thrilled by a wagon-load of harlots, scared by Swabian mercenaries, jobless soldiers of the Holy Roman Empire. I envied noblemen in their luxuriant, ruthless meanderings and, peopling them with my own characters, have been wandering the roads ever since.

A few years later the ageing Lion Feuchtwanger and Heinrich Mann, author of *The Blue Angel*, would be braving the Pyrenees, fleeing from Nazi occupied France, eventually reaching America. My second novel, *Enemies*, owed something to this episode. Published in 1947, it was set in wartime France and Germany – not in the 1940s, however, but in 1870. Little read, it has two curious footnotes. First, although written before I had read *War and Peace*, it features a lumpish, yearning character called Pierre, who ends as a partisan fighting the Germans, and of whom I wrote a longish passage virtually identical to Tolstoy's description of Pierre Bezukhov. Second, in 1991, long after the unsold copies of *Enemies* had been pulped, a letter arrived from Germany in which an unknown man asked permission to adopt me as his heir, requesting in return that I copy out for him any passage from the book.

Written in wartime, *Enemies* is sympathetic to Germans and was partly a riposte to Robert Vansittart's dictum of 1941: 'The hard fact is that 80 per cent of the German race are the political and moral scum of the earth.' A lover of French culture, Robert had published a booklet, *Black Record*, which attributed to the Germans almost all the vileness suffered in Europe since the breakdown of the Roman republic. Goebbels commented in 1943: 'This fellow Vansittart has published a new book of hate ... he is really worth his weight in gold for our propaganda. After the war a monument should be erected to him with the inscription, "to the Englishman who rendered the greatest service to the German cause during the War".'

I retained some of my earlier romanticism, detached from the realities of Holocaust and barbarism – a vision of lonely mountains, peaks glimmering above mist, pointing upwards to invisible goals, always out to reach, in what V.S. Pritchett, writing of *Dr Zhivago*, has called a nostalgia for the future. As a corrective to sentimental waffle, I wrote another novel, *The Friends of God* (1963), set in sixteenth-century Münster, where the fanatical Anabaptists set themselves to destroy Empire and Papacy, denounced the Pope and Luther as two halves of the same bum, abolished private property and monogamy and hailed their leader, Jan van Leyden, as King of the World. In this I could take a cool look at themes of obsession with final truths, the lure of both saviours and destruction, embodied in the handsome, lustful, messianic Jan, who intrigued Bernard Shaw and dominates Meyerbeer's opera *The Prophet*.

A wife-murderer, enchanted by his own oratory, freeing himself from ancient concepts of good and evil, Jan thinks less in words than in tunes, arias, anthems; he prefers pure sensation to the fatigues of hard work, marries many wives, out of lust or curiosity. In his gigantic effort towards extremes, this legendary, demonic figure sets a trap for Germans centuries ahead:

> The real kings were those who never existed. They drift over us in a song, on a stage, at an altar. There never was a heaven or hell, but people wanted them so much that they had to be. I can see incredible distances, even a stone or cloud can show me extraordinary things. Who else in the German Empire can imagine all that I can and without any effort? For me, a blank strip of parchment is worth more than any masterpiece. Sometimes the soul rains, it blackens and stinks, I know this too. And listen. Even Christ was not entirely God, he was not quite convinced. He had a plan for living and a plan for dying, it was too planned, he did not wholly trust himself or God. But I don't have to plan, I have only to stand still, absolutely still. And if I mock only in a whisper, still no one can mock louder than I.

Much later I was sneered at in print for having written about so ridiculous a subject. This was curious, for my critic was a Mrs Osborne, whose late husband, John Osborne, had written his moving play, *Luther*, about Jan's foremost enemy.

Only at around twenty-five did I begin to be seriously aware of style. My own style was still, pompous, verbose, top-heavy, but I was edging towards something more unsensational, oblique, ironic, and had enjoyed P.G. Wodehouse's dedication, in a volume of golfing stories: 'To my daughter Leonora, without whose never-failing sympathy and encouragement this book would have been finished in half the time.' I envied the gentle ironies of L.H. Myers, in his *Strange Glory* from 1936:

> Mr Berkeley Pell was great in such a very superior fashion that comparatively few people had ever heard of him . . . although he was one of the most hard-working and public-spirited men in the whole country, the newspapers never, never printed his name. Sometimes Mr Berkeley Pell took on even heavier responsibilities; sometimes, if approached with sufficient discretion, he would give advice. To the President, to a gathering of the world's greatest bankers, or even to a European state that found itself in difficulties, Mr Berkeley Pell would on occasion speak a few quiet words.

Amid fags and prefects, beaks and footballers, I would have enjoyed speaking those few quiet words, at the cost of never being named in newspapers.

Myers, the son of F.W.H. Myers, a founder of the Society of Psychical Research, was one of the few contemporary writers recognized by the Leavises. Though Marxist-inclined, he was rich, a partner in the West End restaurant Boulestins and a generous, though anonymous benefactor to his fellow-Etonian George Orwell. During the war Orwell, as literary editor of *Tribune*, occasionally gave me a book to review; but, though grateful, I found him too enigmatic and teasing to like much. In my ignorance, however, I felt that all literary editors were worthy of the deepest respect. I was once delivering copy at the old *Tribune* offices,

222 Strand, when Myers appeared, bony-faced, spare and neat, and invited Orwell and myself to dine with him at the great restaurant. In a year of meagre rations and watered beer my eagerness to comply must have irritated Orwell, who emphatically declined for both of us, afterwards, only half-humourously, muttering about black-market grouse and pansy liquor.

Orwell's tastes were certainly ignored at Boulestins. He praised England for new potatoes, mint sauce, marmalade, beer and brown bread. I remember, some time later, remarking to Mr Orwell – I always thought of him as 'Mr'; he was, however reluctantly, the officer, tall, upright, brusque – that Myers was surely due for some official honour. The rasp in his grunt of reply I only fully understood forty years later; examining old numbers of *Tribune*, I found his column, 'As I Please':

> Looking at the photographs in the New Year's Honours List, I am struck (as usual) by the quite exceptional ugliness and vulgarity of the faces displayed there. It seems to be almost the rule that the kind of person who earns the right to call himself Lord Percy de Falcontowers should look at best like an overfed publican, or at worst like a tax-collector with a duodenal ulcer.

Myers' civil servant exterior belied his fiction, his concern with philosophic debate, a search for spirituality and, like Orwell, a rejection of his class, though perhaps even less successfully achieved.

This, however, was still in the future. At school in 1937 history was swirling around us. 'The long-lost dollar come back to the fold,' radio voices sang. Roosevelt flashed smiles like dollar-bills, and, in Germany, a master, organizer of the college Christian Union, told us most interesting things were happening. We read his translation of Hitler Youth songs:

> Behind the leader that we know
> We work with spade and pick and hoe,
> The road to peace he'll surely know.
> The love we all give the State

Shall bury deep all lingering hate.
We of the Ems reclaim waste land,
By wind and sun our bodies tanned,
Standing knee-deep in weed and slime,
Soaked to the skin we tame the Rhine.

Few of us were tempted to stand in the slime. *Mein Kampf*, now in the college library, proved dreary stuff, although I did not then realize that the English edition had been shrewdly doctored.

Daily I read of pacts, settlements, conferences, treaties – treaties which, Goering later explained, he regarded as so much toilet paper. The Rome–Berlin Axis was bawled to trumpet and drum; wars tore China, Spain, the Chaco. Ethiopia was, in the old Roman euphemism, pacified. At home, jokers hummed:

Who's that coming down the street?
Mrs Simpson's sweating feet.
She's been married twice before,
Now she's knocking at Eddy's door.

After the Windsors' marriage, Shaw said he could think of no one better equipped to be queen than someone who had been three times through the mill.

I loved Hollywood musicals, gangster antics, bouncy Broadway tunes. In musicals, slang was transformed to dazzling patterns, in mindless acrobatics of lovely youth pledged to the plush close-up and the happy ending. I crooned, tunelessly:

Her father is a millionaire,
And he has no son and heir,
That's why I want a love-affair
    With Miss Elizabeth Brown.

I was Cagney, I was Astaire, I was Edward G. I swamped myself with Ginger Rogers, Betty Field, Barbara Stanwyck with her long stride and voice like a claw. I began envying the British expatriates in Hollywood; even lack of talent, I thought, might not have debarred me, while the ugliness that still oppressed me might have qualified me if not for King Kong's younger brother at least for George Raft's aide, Alice Faye's agent or one of the bruised thugs who cluster round boxers. I lacked, however, the charm of Colman, the cold glitter of Rathbone, the vast presence of Laughton or the imperturbable nastiness of Sanders – 'the trouble was, we were both in love with George,' Zsa Zsa Gabor said, after their divorce.

Any theatrical ambitions were, however, swiftly obliterated. My performance as a deaf and dumb hag in *The Tales of Hoffmann* was overlooked; not so my antics in a college production of *Caesar and Cleopatra*. As Apollodorus, my lines included the cool assertion, 'Centurion, I am not a merchant, I am a patrician and a votary of art.' Nervousness, however, impelled me to quaver, 'I am centuries old, I am Patricia, a tart from the vortex.' The applause was noisy but discouraging. In the audience was Miss Elsie Fogarty, founder of the Central School of Speech and Drama, who afterwards gave her very favourable opinion of the enterprise until ending, in a clear, firm voice: 'I did not think much of Apollodorus.'

I hastened back to books and my private self. Certain phrases were incantations: 'the Great Gate of Kiev', 'Chancellor of the Spanish Burgundies'. Mirages were evoked by 'Indian hill station', 'Federated Malay States', 'China Seas', 'the High Veldt'. A cracked road sign, 'To the North', made me quake with daring anticipations. 'Light cavalry' still suggests early morning gallops over crisply autumned pastures, a patina of youth and freedom that I was to find in Tolstoy's *The Cossacks*.

Easy-going and tolerant, school allowed many opportunities for stories, explorings and fruitful misunderstandings. A master lent me Lucretius, who articulated much that I had already wordlessly, dimly apprehended:

> Bodies again,
> are partly primal germs and partly
> unions, deriving from the primal germs,

     and those which are the primal germs of things
     no power can quench, for in the end they conquer
     by their own solidity.

I cautiously called an obstructive prefect 'P.G.'. He assumed I meant 'Profusely Gifted', but it was of course 'Primal Germ'.

Lucretius was unmentioned in chapel, but I enjoyed Gospel readings, hymns, organ voluntaries, even an occasional sermon. With more religious temperament than belief, I have always been concerned with the Gospels, irritated by their gaps, contradictions and doubtless errors or ambiguities of translation. Jesus' summary rejection of family, national and treasury values was exciting, but the telling was incomplete. Certain parables were perplexing, leading me to suspect that the early Church, sternly suppressing unwelcome witnesses and writings, distinguished between the élite and the herd. Mark was suggestive: 'To you the secret of the Kingdom of God has been given; but to those on the outside, all is revealed by parables, so that, as the Scriptures declare, they may look, look again, but see nothing at all; they may hear, hear again, but understand nothing, otherwise they might turn to God and be forgiven.'

Did I possess the secret? Not yet. Not ever, though my novels often centred on this dichotomy of initiates and ignorant. I learnt to appreciate Auden's belief that dogma was a shaggy dog story. There was a point, but whoever strove to reach it would miss it.

First World War novels, poems, memoirs were also much in evidence, and the streets were still darkened by gaunt, beribboned beggars, often blind, pleading and sometimes threatening. I thus assumed that everyone, more especially writers and artists, axiomatically hated war and felt shocked incredulity when, preparing a speech for the college debating society, I chanced upon Thomas Mann's 1915 *Thoughts on War*:

The world of peace which has now collapsed with such shattering thunder – did we not all of us have enough of it? Was it not foul with all its comfort? Did it not fester and stink with the decomposition of civilization? Morally and psychologically, I felt the necessity of the catastrophe and that feeling, elevation and liberation, which filled me, when what one had thought impossible actually happened.

A German novelist once recalled to me how Mann periodically gave dinners as a preliminary to reading aloud some completed work. At table would be those he recognized as his peers: Hermann Hesse, perhaps; Gerhart Hauptmann, maybe. Allowed in afterwards were smaller fry – the Feuchtwangers, Wassermanns, Alfred Neumanns. Then, permitted nothing but the master's voice, were those whom Mann scarcely thought of as writers, such as Aldous Huxley.

Writers can be misleadingly credited with exceptional human sympathies. An acclaimed dramatist once outlined for me his latest play, with lengthy quotation, the women's speeches delivered in a falsetto that could have cracked a window. After some hours I was distracted by actual cries from the bedroom above and realized that – at best – his girl must be suffering a miscarriage. I risked an interruption, pointing upwards. The writer nodded: 'Gosh, that gives me the missing scene!'

Meanwhile, the dictators were cavorting in the mummeries of gangster power. Like many others, I was momentarily awed. Looking back, however, I see thirties Europe more as a nursery where the adults played with toys too big for them, the children laughed and wondered, while below the floor the flames – terrible playfellows – had started. After the Soviet show trials of the period, André Malraux announced that Stalin gave dignity to humanity; and respectable English were admiring Mussolini, guarantor of order. Wyndham Lewis, the country's foremost modernist had, in 1926, proposed a revived Holy Roman Empire, comprising Britain, Italy and France, with Mussolini as emperor. A few years later, in 1932, Robert Atkins produced at the New Theatre *Napoleon: The Hundred Days* by Mussolini, who proclaimed himself the most intelligent animal who had ever existed. The great poet Rilke wrote of Il Duce: 'What soaring of language, and not only in literature but in politics', while Jung endorsed him as 'an original man of good taste'.

Italian savagery in Ethiopia, however, gave no credence for that good taste. Mussolini's airman son exulted in the sport of gunning down and bombing defenceless villages. I was tearful during a newsreel of the small, dignified black Emperor of Ethiopia, Haile Selassie, appealing to the League of Nations while fascist sympathizers hooted and whistled.

Denis Mack Smith wrote of Il Duce in his *Mussolini* (1981):

> A well-organized claque followed him around to be present at his speeches – the applause squad it was sometimes called – and a system of bells and prompt cards helped to produce the appropriate action . . . School teachers were ordered to magnify this solitary figure, to stress his disinterestedness, his wonderful courage and brilliant mind, and to teach that obedience to such a man was the highest virtue. His picture, often in one of his Napoleonic poses, was displayed on all public buildings and could sometimes be carried in procession through the streets like the image of a patron saint . . . He was compared to Aristotle, Kant and Aquinas: he was the greatest genius in Italian history, greater than Dante or Michelangelo, greater than Washington, Lincoln or Napoleon: he was, in fact, a god.

Mussolini had travelled far from his youth, when, as a socialist teacher and journalist, he had thirteen times dodged military service in the First World War, had yelled that the national flag was a rag to plant on a dunghill. By 1945, his stuffing was gone; he was left hanging upside down in a Milan square, and at Templecombe Station I saw '*Finito Benito*' chalked on a packing case.

Mussolini, Rienzi, Nero. Hitler, Jan van Leyden. Clearly, history was as much a maze as an evolutionary progress, the past endlessly recycled by buffoons, paranoiacs, desperados carving out their own names at whatever cost. Progress ebbed and flowed; I was never to lose sight of the giant theme of the barbarians on the frontier, the defensive walls that defend so little, atavism, the beckoning of the irrational.

In 1933 the Reichstag fire trial had convulsed Europe. Communists faced capital charges for arson. For myself, here was a simple confrontation of good and evil, like a fairy-tale. The hero was the Bulgarian Georgi Dimitrov, who repeatedly challenged Hermann Goering, in words that electrified: 'Are you, by any chance, afraid of my questions, Herr Minister-President?' He reduced his furious accuser to scarlet-faced, turkey-cock incoherence and, against all odds, secured acquittal for himself and the others. Dimitrov departed to Russia. The story was, however, not quite finished. Dimitrov was now the beloved of all free men; Goering, First World War flying ace, drug addict, thief, fantasist, was the founder of the Gestapo, first instigator of the Final Solution and incompetent air force boss. An Austrian communist, Ernst Fischer, subsequently met Dimitrov in Moscow, where he had lapsed into a Stalinist dummy, as Comintern Secretary, and later a toadying premier of postwar Bulgaria. Confidentially, he told Fischer a story that appeared only in Fischer's 1974 autobiography, *An Opposing Man*:

> After my clash with Goering, the guards were more forthcoming than they had ever been before; one of them gave my shoulder a friendly nudge while the other would have been only too pleased to shake my hand. Well satisfied, I lay down in my cell with the feeling that I was going to have a good night. And then the unexpected happened: noises and heavy footsteps, the door was flung open, the guard stood to attention and Goering walked in. A bull going to gore me with his horns in revenge for the defeat in the court-room? With his legs astraddle, he stood staring at me, then suddenly held out his hand: 'Pity you're an enemy! But it's men like you one needs as one's friends.'

In 1939 Leonard Woolf published the aptly titled *Barbarians at the Gate*. In college vacations I saw many new, foreign faces and read that Britain was waiving passport regulations for child refugees, accepting 10,000 from Germany. Former Prime Minister Stanley Baldwin's gramophone record appeal for Jewish Relief collected £250,000. As I wandered the streets I felt myself more than ever surrounded by a tapestry from which stiff, dramatic beings – vivid but never wholly real – were about to step down and challenge me. I was learning the mystique of frontiers, the atmosphere changing abruptly between 'Street', 'Crescent', 'Drive'; between late afternoon and dusk, when a child might meet a lisping killer; fissures of Europe, joining the boundaries of class and the separation of I and They. I watched half-opened doors, curtains hastily drawn; near Baker Street, in the unbidden stillness of a certain mews, there was always a long black car with darkened windows. I was not surprised when, during the war, an actor stalked unaccosted through London in full SS uniform, people scarcely glancing at him, soldiers of many nations unconcerned. Certain areas were thick with idle, enigmatic youths, lounging, smoking, saying nothing as I passed, but with eyes I felt menacing me from behind – youths of whom Mervyn Peake wrote:

> I see them at the cold, accepted wall,
> The trouser-pocket boys, the cocky walkers.

Outside the Haverstock Arms a large, mottled man beckoned me: 'Have this on me, lad.' He was soon telling me of a special saddle made for the Duke of Wellington. 'He'd the beginnings of a tail, as you've probably learnt at some fancy school.'

I had not, but my own stories still floated through me. Listen. A butler stands behind the father's chair as the family dines. He is smiling, pleased with them, even more pleased with himself, for has he not poisoned the lot? Reading that the German headsmen performed in dinner-jacket, spats and white gloves, and that one was a popular ballroom dancing instructor, I imagined *The Handsome Executioner*, in which local authorities appoint a headsman to reduce crime, but, besotted by his glamour, people queue to denounce themselves, eager for his axe.

At eighteen I had seen Fritz Lang films, had read widely but in easy enough terrain, was ignorant of *The Waste Land*, *Dubliners*, *A Draft of Thirty Cantos* as I was of Cubism and atonalism. Like a sheriff in a western I seemed always arriving late. Early Auden, with its mountain fastnesses, mysterious passes, secret agents, jazzy images and unexpected rhythms, cocksure teachings, grasped me by the throat. In *Voltaire at Fennay*, he wrote:

> Yes, the fight
> Against the false and the unfair
> Was always worth it. So was gardening. Civilize.

To remedy my ignorance, and to meet the famous, the beautiful, the sophisticated, I paid half-a-crown to join the Senior North London Literary Circle where, surely, I would scarcely be able to avoid chats with H.G. Wells, Edwin and Willa Muir, J.B. Priestley, Rose Macaulay, C.E.M. Joad. In this I was disappointed. The members, all, in my view, elderly, were not of the finest quality, their talk only marginally literary.

'Betjeman's still in Chelsea.'

'They say he has a poisoned toe.'

'I did see La Sitwell?'

'False nose?'

'She doesn't need to.'

'I only got Kathleen. She's like a building society, you're expected to put a bit in, then watch it grow. She still thinks D.H. Lawrence knew how to write.'

I wondered about the advantages of the Junior North London Literary Circle.

My early world, however, was about to end; first, with my winning a major history scholarship to Oxford, which made me resolve not to be only a story-teller but also a Major Historian. Second, with Britain's declaration of war in September 1939; in the opinion of Molotov, Stalin's Foreign Minister: 'The British Government has announced that its aim in the war with Germany is nothing more or less than the destruction of Hitlerism. There is no justification for a war of this kind.'

Molotov's signing of the Nazi–Soviet non-aggression pact in August had at once destroyed my radical convictions, though I was combating Bernard Shaw's verdict, that he alone had the sense to recognize that Hitler was now under Stalin's thumb. I heard my favourite actor, Michael Redgrave, address the anti-war People's Convention, maintaining that, with the great Stalin now allied with Hitler and Himmler, a guarantee had been enforced against a British police state; a deposition had been levied against British imperialism, and the survival of human decency was now underwritten. The unsavoury American ambassador, Joseph Kennedy, soon reported with some relish to Roosevelt Britain's imminent collapse.

Already debarred from physical conflict by those unexplained faints I could only murmur the refrain of the old Anglo-Saxon poem 'Deor': 'All that passed away. So may this.'

2
DISTANT PLANETS

If you cannot read all your books, at any rate handle, or, as it were, fondle them – peer into them, let them fall open where they will, read from them the first sentence that arrests the eye, set them back on the shelves with your own hands, arrange them on your own plan, so that if you do not know them to be your friends, let them at any rate be your acquaintances. If they cannot enter the circle of your life, do not deny them at least a nod of recognition.

– Winston Churchill

Anybody can make history. Only a great man can write it. There is no mode of action, no form of emotion that we do not share with the lower animals. It is only by language that we rise above them – by language, which is the parent, not the child, of thought.

– Oscar Wilde

PRE-WAR authors still possessed public eminence. In a single year H.G. Wells addressed the Sorbonne, the Weimar Reichstag, the Petrograd Soviet; interviewed Stalin, met Theodore Roosevelt and dined with F.D.R. 'Wellsian', like 'Shavian', had global significance.

Until my twenties, published writers were for me distant planets, Grand Impossibles, inhabiting a further dimension, a more exalted metaphor, like the demi-gods in de Chirico's surrealist novel, *Hebdomeros*, who go into the sea in order not to get wet. Their panache, their resilience, encouraged me; their books, like rural footpaths, were lasting reminders of life's inconsistencies and deceptions, a humorous devil afoot in the universe, mingling the beautiful, wild and strange.

In 1938 Winston Churchill was someone I regarded primarily as a writer and as an extinct politician entangled in lost causes. Though, one heard, prone to melancholy, he possessed the gusto of an earlier age: Johnson, Wilkes, Fox, Palmerston, W.G. Grace. He had told the pacifist

Labour minister Arthur Ponsonby that he liked things to happen and, that if they did not, he liked to make them happen. A.G. Gardiner, the Liberal journalist, remembered him as always in a hurry with the delight of a boy at a fair. He 'thanked the high gods for the gift of existence'. Enjoying authority, he did not make it readily identified with pain. As Prime Minister he protested against the five years' penal servitude inflicted on a woman for telling two soldiers that Hitler was a good ruler and a better man than Mr Churchill.

He had been young in an age of wonder: the New Science, Art, Psychology, Woman; he had mixed with Distant Planets, not always to best effect. Leon Edel has described an interlude at Walmer Castle, where guests included the First Lord of the Admiralty, Churchill, and the Master, Henry James:

> the two most articulate men present. Churchill, full of pride, confidence, faith and swagger, found Henry James at the centre. The First Lord had never read James, he was impatient at the deference shown to the old man who was so slow a-spoken, even though his rhetoric was so remarkable – when he finally got it out: Churchill disregarded the Master; or he interrupted him. He showed him no conversational consideration. He used a great deal of slang, some of which apparently grated on the novelist.

Yet the Master posthumously won the brash politician's perhaps unwitting recognition, when, as wartime leader, Churchill broadcast a tribute to 'this decent and dauntless people', the words of the expatriate Henry James.

At college, reading Churchill's biography of Marlborough, I took it for a masterpiece, though this was questionable. For Evelyn Waugh,

> As history, it is beneath contempt, the special pleading of a defence lawyer. As literature it is worthless. It is written in a sham Augustan prose which could only have been written by a man who thought always in terms of public speech, and the antitheses clang, like hammers on an anvil.

Churchill indeed had Augustan qualities, but the modernist art critic Herbert Read, lover of Wordsworth, guide through Western art for many of us, thought the eighteenth century silly, selfish, complacent, and Churchill did not escape his disdain. In his *English Prose Style* he judged his writing falsely dramatic and self-promoting, the images stale, the metaphors violent.

The biographer Michael Holroyd later repeated an anecdote of Lytton Strachey remembering, to Dora Carrington, that he had met Churchill at a pre-1939 dinner: 'I talked to him a good deal. Do you know, in spite of everything I couldn't help liking him. H.G. Wells says very much the same in *Men Like Gods* (1923): one somehow can't dislike the poor creature. He was delighted when I said that I thought his book [*The World Crisis: 1911–1914*] very well done, and hardly seemed to mind when I added I also thought it was very wicked.'

'H.G.' himself fared worse; 'I stopped thinking about him when he became a thinker,' said Strachey.

In boyhood, I had understood that Churchill aroused more respect than affection. Robert Vansittart supported him in his wilderness years, and later perhaps hoped from him more than he received. Most adults seemed to rate him bumptious, unscrupulous and of poor judgement. 'Winston,' Robert Boothby declared, years afterwards, 'was a shit, but we needed a shit to defeat Hitler.' A Conservative elder, J.C.C. Davidson, wrote: 'Churchill is the sort of man whom, if I wanted a mountain to be moved, I would send for at once. I think, however, that I would not consult him after he had removed the mountain, if I wanted to know where to put it.'

I was to be astounded when, after the war was over, the military experts Basil Liddell Hart and General J.F.C. Fuller grandly rebuked Churchill for his unwisdom in rejecting Hitler's peace offers in 1940, thus assuring the loss of the British Empire.

Hitler himself is unlikely to have assessed Churchill's books, remarking in 1942:

If we look at our enemies, we see this gabbler, this drunkard Churchill. What has he done all his life? This hypocritical fellow! This first-class lazybones! Posterity will speak of Churchill only as the destroyer of an Empire, destroyed by him, not us. Churchill has said that I wanted war – and a small clique with him. Behind this drunken clique stand the paymaster Jews.

Stalin was more temperate, telling the Yugoslav delegate to a Moscow conference, the writer and partisan fighter Milovan Djilas: 'Churchill is the type who will pick a kopeck from your pocket if you don't watch him! And Roosevelt? Roosevelt is different. He thrusts in his hand only for the larger coins. But Churchill! Churchill will do it for a kopeck!'

Whatever his deficiencies of character, of literary subtlety, Churchill's pungency was unflagging. He compared de Gaulle to a female llama surprised in her bath; John Foster Dulles to a bull carrying his own china shop. Isaiah Berlin has mentioned Churchill's response to a 1940 Foreign Office draft about soundings taken, behind his back and through Swedish diplomats, concerning possible peace negotiations with Hitler: 'The ideas set forth appeared to me to err in trying to be too clever, to enter into refinements of policy unsuited to the tragic simplicity and grandeur of the times and the issues at stake.'

This would not have impressed my exact contemporary Alex Comfort, pacifist, doctor, poet and novelist of precocious and enviable talents, who published a long, anti-Churchill diatribe in wartime *Tribune*:

> You've heard His Nibs decanting year by year
>   The dim production of his bulldog brain,
> While homes and factories sit to hear
>   The same old drivel dished up once again.

Multitudes in suffering Europe would have expressed it differently.

A.J.P. Taylor, no devotee of stock heroes, thought Churchill the penalty people paid for reading history, yet regarded him as remarkable leader, with great mistakes, great achievements. Progressive, resentful, sometimes mischievous but always interesting, his early radicalism – with Lloyd George he pioneered the Welfare State – derived from 'a warm-hearted desire to benefit the poor and oppressed.' Isaiah Berlin wrote in 1949:

> Churchill's dominant category, the simple, central, organizing principle of his moral and intellectual universe is a historical imagination so strong, so comprehensive, as to encase the whole of the present and the whole of the future in a rich and multi-coloured past. Such an approach is dominated by a desire – and a capacity – to find moral and intellectual bearings, to give shape and character and direction and coherence to the stream of events.

When in 1965 the mighty dockland cranes dipped in salute to the river launch carrying Churchill's coffin, I wept freely. More mundane feelings revived next day, when my mother asserted that the mechanics had demanded extra payment.

Another of my Distant Planets at this time was George Bernard Shaw. In his book *Great Contemporaries*, Churchill called Bernard Shaw a Jack Frost, nimble and sparkling, tracing patterns exquisite but ephemeral, leading nowhere. Later, Shaw's biographer Michael Holroyd judged that he preserved the invariable politeness of readability, was extraordinarily skilful at placing his facts and figures in a human context and, whenever possible, conjured entertainment from them.

All this early attracted me to the gyrations of the inescapable G.B.S., as I might be to a dancer of unpredictable fancies performing to unheard music, always out of reach but with a magnetism that enchanted, and was somehow on my side against the heavy, dull and predictable. V.S. Pritchett has written: 'The Irish are almost always shy, almost always try to conceal, and they have notoriously been apt to produce a stage personality to do so.' Hesketh Pearson had already related an incident supporting this, suggesting another Shaw behind the sprightly G.B.S.

> His love of clowning, an effervescence of vitality, led many unimaginative people to believe that he was usually talking with his tongue in his cheek; and even his unrehearsed effects had an irritant quality because his natural shyness made him appear extraordinarily cool. One day at

Westminster Bridge underground station he slipped at the top of the stairs and shot down the whole flight on his back, while the onlookers held their breath in horror. Then he rose to his feet without the least surprise and walked on as if that were his usual way of going downstairs. The shriek of laughter from the onlookers expressed relief, annoyance and mirth in about equal proportions.

Shaw wrote to T.E. Lawrence in 1923: 'I am naturally a pitiably nervous, timid man, born with a whole plume of white feathers, but nowadays this only gives a zest to the fun of swanking at every opportunity.'

Shaw followed Lord Berners' thesis that in Anglo-Saxon countries art is more highly appreciated if accompanied by a certain measure of eccentric publicity. For himself, Shaw was a 'sort of Bishop of Everywhere'. He had theories, often preposterous, about statecraft, economics, medicine, religion, education and, increasingly, the necessity for authority and the virtues of dictators, stemming from his own Caesar. 'They always make out that Stalin is a grim, dull kind of tyrant: I assure you, we'll soon know him for what he is, a statesman of unique experience, and, what is most important, I found him to have a sense of humour.'

After a visit to Russia, Shaw declared, 'As far as I could make out, the prisoners could stay in camps as long as they liked', and after Hitler invaded Austria he wrote: 'His book made a favourable impression on me, though it is a great pity that he had not read my books instead of Houston Chamberlain.'

After the war he met another vain man, Field-Marshal Montgomery, and doubtless lectured him on the deficiencies of the military mind. Montgomery described him as an intensely compacted hank of steel wire. Wells gibed that Shaw was a chaos of clear ideas. For Ezra Pound, fascistic sneerer at F.D.R. as 'Mr Jewsevelt', he was 'a ninth-rate coward'. However, throughout my somewhat prolonged youth, Shaw's clear-cut prose was invigorating and instructive. *The Adventures of the Black Girl in Search of God* gave me an encapsulation of biblical concepts, as a fluid, evolutionary progress from superstition to humanism: his 'Life Force' –

ceaselessly, impersonally experimenting, testing, discarding, failing with a dinosaur, succeeding with a Schweitzer, or Chekhov – was more plausible than the school chapel God, omnipotent and loving, but creating a world of hatred and conflict, a God thought all too personal, motivated by loneliness, curiosity, perhaps caprice, even malice, compressed into Hardy's question:

> Has some Vast Imbecility
> Mighty to build and blend
> But impotent to lend
> Framed us in jest, and left us now to hazardry?

I was beginning to imagine God as 'It', woven into the evolutionary process, still self-creating, not yet complete. What then excited me in Shaw was the freedom he personified. Years before Sartre he taught that we could remake ourselves, reach beyond habit, inherited traits and values. He did not wallow in tragedy and bemoan the human condition; he defined unpleasant circumstances and proposed remedies. That the diagnosis could be crude, the remedies often ludicrous, I seldom then realized: for me, the performance was superb. Meanwhile, I did know that evil, like virtue, could be chosen, not inherited. Only occasionally, a moment in a play might arouse my misgivings, identifying it, not, as I subsequently learnt, wholly unreasonably, with Shaw himself.

> PICKERING: Does it occur to you, Higgins, that the girl has some feelings?
> HIGGINS: Oh no, I don't think so. Not any feelings we need bother about.

This attitude I was to find fairly common amongst political thinkers. My loyalty to Shaw had ample cause to waver during later years: T.S. Eliot told Colin Wilson that he found Shaw unreadable; A.J.P. Taylor attacked 'the vain old charlatan', and Joyce called him a mountebank. When Rebecca West's *Black Lamb and Grey Falcon* was published, an Indian accosted me:

'Hey! You know Mr George B. Shaw?'

'No, I do not.'

'No care. I have to write to him and tell him he is mentioned in Miss West's new book.'

'Well, I don't think . . .'

The Indian was stern. 'I must inform him that he is mentioned in Miss West's new book.'

Later I looked up the reference. It was indeed there.

Rebecca West complained that Shaw had too few ideas and those he did have were bad ones:

> Wells at least had an idea that people would have ideas if they were taught by other people who had some, and he was almost as sublime a controversialist as Voltaire when he met an irrational fool, but Shaw stands for nothing but a socialism which has nothing to it except a belief that it would be a nicer world if everybody were clean and well fed, which is based on no analysis of man and depends on no theory of the state and an entirely platitudinous denunciation of hypocrisy which nowhere rises to the level of Tartuffe.

Yet behind it all I could nevertheless imagine a man aged but still cheerful, still on the attack, though incapable of cruelty even to a walnut, and who, if asked a question, would at once reply, disconcertingly, teasingly, often so obviously wrong that it deflected us into ways of thought unexpected and, therefore, illuminating.

I once attended a crowded, enthusiastic debate between Shaw and Wells, enthralled, like everyone else, by Shaw's charm, fluent inexactitudes and courteous, smiling patience with Wells' exasperation. For Wells, Shaw spoke glibly but was incurably muddle-headed, taking for granted the 'licensed murder' of vaccination, the monstrous sham of 'that foolish gabble-shop' Parliament, the omniscience of Stalin.

Wells knew that he himself was an unimpressive speaker but always in the right. 'Mr Shaw is one of those perpetual children who live in a dream of make-believe, and that make-believe of Mr Shaw is that he is a person of incredible wisdom and subtlety running the world. He is an elderly adolescent still at play. To understand that is a clue to all Shavianism.' In return, Shaw thought that Wells taught everything and learnt nothing.

After the war, Kathleen Raine, a poet with a vision which penetrated the smooth surfaces of natural beauty to expose the more intricate designs beneath, listed the twentieth century's most important writers, omitting Shaw and Wells, though not herself. Initially, I was indignant but now understand better. Their self-assured trust in reason, their assertive generalizations, their vulgarizing fine writing by journalistic insertions and stale debates, invited what Arnold Toynbee was calling the idealization of a dead self, the nemesis of creativity. The recent genocidal horrors made much of their panache seem irrelevant or worse. In old age, Shaw told his neighbour, Stephen Winsten: 'War, disease and starvation had always been accepted until I came upon the scene. It won't be very long when dying of illness will be rare and starvation, disease and war will be thought unnatural and be declared crimes.'

Nevertheless, while many friends were mysteriously idolizing Sartre and Brecht, I remained grateful to Shaw, whom I considered had taught the gist of their thought years previously. He could still attract the young, including the polymathic Colin Wilson, the philosopher and novelist Bryan Magee and the late novelist Brigid Brophy, who said that she owed her ability to write English prose to her father and his advice to read Evelyn Waugh and Bernard Shaw.

In many ways, however, H.G. Wells was of more immediate consequence to me. He was foremost in demonstrating that history did not begin in East Sussex in 1066 but among the rocks and shallow seas millennia ago, that the universe itself was not a glittering muddle but subject to laws, vibrating with evolutionary possibilities. His *Outline of History* and *A Short History of the World* gave me new words that stretched my imagination like rubber – Lower Palaeozoic, Eoanthropus, Neanderthal – complementing his book titles: *Men Like Gods, The First Men in the Moon, When the Sleeper Awakes, The Undying Fire, The Discovery of the Future, The Research Magnificent, A Modern Utopia* . . . all promising adventure, movement, optimism, the overcoming of Time, Space, Ignorance, Disease.

The Outline was rated by A.J.P. Taylor the most acceptable of universal histories, and Isherwood thought it a masterpiece. It directly inspired my 1990 novel *The Wall*. I was excited by Wells' image of a postage stamp placed beneath Nelson's Column: the thickness of the stamp represented the past; the distance between the stamp and Nelson's hat the future. Like Churchill and Shaw, he encouraged by his gusto, rather than dispirited by introspective despair. The three galvanized me, with what Henry James called the easy impudence of genius.

Today Wells seems slapdash in his prejudices, writing in *The Shape of Things to Come* that Nazism was 'essentially Jewish in spirit and origin', though he would gleefully have produced Old Testament instances of apartheid, genocide, evictions. He was no more enthusiastic than Shaw about the Common Man; they both desired the Uncommon Man, to join up with themselves, ushering in, inhabiting the Perfect State. The coarse facts of boarding school life, and some of Wells' own short stories, had, however, early immunized me against utopias. We should doubtless work for them, as for the principles of the Sermon on the Mount, though I neither believed in them nor desired them. Perfection resembles absolute Freedom: impossible, but useful as a goal, provided that haste for it does not provoke intolerance and cruelty. The German socialist Rosa Luxemburg had written that a man hurrying to do a great deed who knocks down a child out of unfeeling carelessness commits a crime. Likewise, we are all in a condemned cell but must behave as if we will die only on our 150th birthday.

Wells never recollected in tranquillity, was always impatient, busy, angry. His perkiness and indomitable grip on life always encouraged me. He told Virginia Woolf that he most admired courage and vitality, undeterred by her response, 'How ghastly!' I was moved when old, virtually finished, he completed his doctoral thesis: 'On the Quality of Illusion in the Continuity of the Individual Life in the Higher Metazoa with particular reference to the species Homo Sapiens'.

Always in the news, though for me another Distant Planet, was Bertrand Russell. He had opposed the First World War, rejected Christianity, had been satirized by Ezra Pound, mixed with Shaw, Wells, Aldous Huxley, Eliot, and, more intimately, with the first Mrs Eliot and with D.H. Lawrence, whose beliefs in blood, passion, instinct and male supremacy he ultimately concluded 'led straight to Auschwitz'. Indeed Lawrence, while tenderly imaginative about birds, beasts, flowers, once wrote to Ottoline Morrell: 'What is death in an individual? I don't care if sixty million individuals die.' During the Cold War period Russell himself was to later to reject pacifism and advocate atomic attack on Russia should Stalin remain obdurate in his unremitting hostility.

Russell was the last British writer to address the entire world; spokesman for the anti-nuclear lobby, pleading for human survival. Small, dapper, white-haired, unscrupulous womanizer, he was instantly recognizable to thousands unconcerned with mathematics and repelled by philosophy. A London taxi driver related: 'One of my passengers was Bertrand Russell. I recognized him, of course, so I said to him: "Well, Lord Russell, what's it all about, eh?" And, do you know, he couldn't tell me!'

Russell, always trenchant, once told Bryan Magee that the Labour hero Aneurin Bevan thought it more important that he should become Foreign Secretary than that the human race should survive, apropos of Bevan renouncing his previous anti-bomb policy. Russell's clarity, logic and restrained invective exhilarated me: they cleared the human jungle. Before the First World War he had complained that a book on birth control for working men's wives had been prohibited because it was understood by working men's wives. Later, in *Education* (1926), he wrote:

> The main causes of unhappiness at present are: ill-health, poverty, and an unsatisfactory sex-life. The last is partly due to bad education, partly due to persecution by the authorities and Mrs Grundy. A generation of women brought up without irrational sex-fears would soon make an end of this. Fear has been thought the only way to make women 'virtuous', and they have been deliberately taught to be cowards, both physically and mentally. Women in whom love is cramped encourage brutality and hypocrisy. One generation of fearless women could transform the world by bringing into it a generation of fearless children, not contorted into unnatural shapes, but straight and candid, generous, affectionate and free. Their ardour would sweep away the cruelty and pain which we endure, because we are lazy, cowardly, half-hearted and stupid.

Today, I am not cynical but more sceptical. Some of my associates, men and women, have been sexually fearless, indeed reckless, yet aggressive and self-destructive; and Mussolini, for example, could not have suffered from an inhibited sex life. The Pill did not axiomatically induce security and happiness. Moreover, to rely on human reason and logic is precarious: a humane, sexually adjusted family can produce a monster.

Millions spent on education have, in fact, created a very ill-educated society – my own school, relatively expensive, left me ignorant of modern languages, mathematics, all branches of science and, despite enforced study of Latin, I still do not know how the Romans said 'yes'. That the fault was largely my own is actually my plea: in their initial ardour, Shaw, Wells and Russell undervalued the elements of unreason, perversity, fashion, bone-laziness in most of us. Most of my favourite writers were scoundrels or at least socially unsatisfactory. Imagine having Dostoevsky to stay for a week, Tolstoy for a fortnight, entrusting one's girlfriend to Voltaire, one's life savings to Balzac, one's reputation to Pope.

The Distant Planets shared a convinction that life had purpose, that evolution was a drama, with periodic set-backs and false starts. I was never, however, to meet them, and would have been paralysed if I had.

By 1941 I had still met no real writers, but an opportunity then occurred. I submitted my first novel to various publishers, who summarily rejected it; finally Chatto and Windus accepted it, on the recommendation of V.S. Pritchett. I was, of course, overjoyed: here was my first real birthday, the start of another life. I was, I thought – presumptuously, erroneously – taking a seat with the immortals, with the unqualified benediction of V.S. Pritchett, whom I had never met but whose work I revered.

V.S. Pritchett was, throughout my adult life, our most versatile man of letters – novelist, biographer, travel writer, critic, journalist, foremost short-story writer and with an autobiographical masterpiece aptly compared to Dickens and the best of Wells. Sir Victor collected many superlatives and honours, but few men were less grandiose; he was ruminative but never garrulous, slightly diffident, always helpful, and with an inexhaustible range of anecdotes, many told wryly against himself. Once, at a *New Statesman* lunch, he sat next to J.B. Priestley, who ignored him for twenty minutes while chewing gustily. Then he spoke: 'I see Pritchett's been made a director.' Mutual silence until, the meal ending, Priestley allowed him further attention. 'I'm resigning.'

Markedly independent, V.S. ignored fashion, reputations, political correctness, once reflecting that the smart set is the quintessential dust bowl, and he saw a perpetual question mark hanging over accepted notions. Nor did he allow personal affection to distort his judgements. From the age of fifteen he worked in Paris as a shop assistant and salesman, in leather, glue, shellac, then as a journalist in Dublin, New York and London, about which he wrote three splendidly idiosyncratic books. He was worldly, in enjoying the world and its variousness, meticulously charting its curious details, singular human encounters, the bizarre secrets beneath normality. Julian Symons wrote that part of Pritchett's art rested on the assumption that ordinary people say and do extraordinary things.

His perceptions were invariably individual; like Orwell, he could reveal what was seen daily but seldom observed. His *London Perceived* compresses a multitude of facts, opinions, quirky asides, keeping the reader constantly alert: 'In London, it is difficult, anywhere, to be more than fifty yards from a tree.' I immediately thought of him on seeing a van labelled 'Porn and Dunwoody' parked outside the London Library, doubtless about to deliver further stock to the Athenaeum.

Son of an improvident, self-important father, V.S. had ample experiences of life's challenges and comedy. In contrast, there was a rootedness about his own composed stockiness, a quiet Cromwellian stubbornness – and indeed he often referred to English puritanism, its grandiloquent hypocrisies, its achievements through dedication, intolerance, hard work. None worked harder than himself: 'I was fanatical about writing, the word and the sentence were my religion.' Unimaginable howling in demos or raging for his rights, he eluded any visible fanaticism through his humour, common sense and knowledge that headlong righteousness induces vapid literature. 'I often wish I had the guts to get into debt. But I have done, given my circumstances and character, what I have been able to do, and I have enjoyed it.' He was, I think, a happy man, fulfilled in his work, his marriage, his children and grandchildren. He knew his worth, without being self-important: 'The views of a novelist are hardly more than the steam rising from a simmering pot.'

Throughout the war, his weekly *New Statesman* 'Books in General' was for thousands a one-man college, introducing rare and suggestive names – Shchedrin, Goncharov, Asakov, Sheridan le Fanu, Lady Murasaki, Eca de Queiroz, while not overlooking Scott, Rider Haggard, Jerome K. Jerome: 'Jerome relies on misleading moral commentary and that understatement which runs like rheumatism through English humour.' Many of his assertions linger; on Arthur Koestler, for example, using words like 'thought-saving gadgets from the iron-mongering counter, [drawing] especially on the vocabulary of science and economics which is paralysed by patents . . . he seldom makes a dull remark but rarely makes one that common experience does not flatly contradict'.

Pritchett's own imagery was always imaginative, seldom fantastic. Defoe's style, 'plain as a yard of cloth', a blue sky, 'bold as a sailor's collar'. Little was unimportant to him; he once said that it is the journalist's business to interview everything. Far more than a journalist himself, he never lost the journalist's scent for the immediate. His story 'Many Are Disappointed' had already set me an example not only of how to manage words but also when best to omit them.

I enjoyed over forty years of his friendship, though I began it foolishly. Delirious with the acceptance of my novel by Chatto, I resisted Harold Raymond's proposal that I should meet Mr Pritchett. He had noticed certain faults in my manuscript, could suggest a few improvements. I was outraged. Faults? There were none. Improvements? Inconceivable. But beneath this tiro conceit was fear; his stories and articles had opened immeasurable vistas but forced me to imagine a vast, authoritarian figure set to demolish my masterpiece. Those who remember V.S. – that twinkling curiosity, those courteous manners – will gape at this absurdity. I thus delayed meeting him for several years, to my loss. Always good company, he was unusual in attracting no malice or innuendo. Since his death in 1997 I have seethed with questions too late to ask him.

3

DETECTIVE STORY

The man you saw – Lob-lie-by-the-fire, Jack Cade,
Jack Smith, Jack Moon, poor Jack of every trade,
Young Jack, or Old Jack, or Jack What-d'ye call,
Jack-in-the-hedge, or Robin-run-by-the-wall,
Robin Hood, Ragged Robin, Lazy Bob,
One of the Lords of No Man's Land, good Lob –
Although he was seen dying at Waterloo,
Hastings, Agincourt, and Sedgemoor too –
Lives yet.

          – Edward Thomas

Truth being, I think, very excusable in a historian.

         – Jane Austen (aged fifteen)

I HAD decided to be a Major Historian, capitalizing a love of history surfacing from illustrated stories, museum paintings, cinema posters, flamboyant mysteries unfinished, indeed scarcely begun. Dragon ships off Pevensey, the Scarlet Pimpernel Sir Percy Blakeney elegantly dodging the guillotine and French cut-throats with quizzing glass and ironic smile, Harold stricken at Hastings under an explosive comet . . . even before I could read, they had me entangled in a web of suggestion.

I became absorbed with books now mostly forgotten, sturdily patriotic, earnestly inaccurate. Lady Calcott's *Little Arthur's History of England*, H.H. Marshall's *Our Island Story*, Agnes Strickland's *Heroes of England and Empire*. The best was Charles Dickens' *A Child's History of England*, racy, slapdash, coarsely prejudiced, vivid with tearing battles, a prolonged execution, royal murder, lilied heroines, stainless heroes, clanking villains. Of this, G.K. Chesterton wrote that the child was not the reader but the writer. He dramatized the already dramatic, gentle reproof was not his way with a Richard III or Monmouth. I relished his assault on James I's favourite and yearned to be a favourite myself.

> The new favourite got on fast. He was made a viscount, he was made Duke of Buckingham, he was made a marquis, he was made Master of the Horse, he was made Lord High Admiral – and the Chief Commander of the gallant English forces that had dispersed the Spanish Armada, was displaced to make room for him. He had the whole kingdom at his disposal, and his mother sold all the profits and honours of the State, as if she had kept a shop. He blazed all over with diamonds and other precious stones, from his hat band and his earrings to his shoes. Yet he was an ignorant presumptuous swaggering compound of knave and fool, with nothing but his beauty and dancing to recommend him.

'Master of the Horse' intrigued me. Was there only one horse? I would never, alas, be a favourite of anyone. My lack of beauty was notorious, my dancing a monotonous stamp. Self-debasement forced me not to wallow in daydreams but to seek further. Reading history eventually made me feel like a detective in a story with plenty of clues, most of them misleading, overlooked, but with no corpse in the library or, if there was a death, it was that of an England largely imagined, fabricated or taken on trust – an England already doomed by new attitudes towards sovereignty, morals, language. A death to be mourned, applauded or scarcely noticed.

At that time classroom history was mostly political – wars, treaties, rulers – leaving me free to explore remote ancestors, their legends, place-names, words, scattered like pollen. As if magnified by Holmes' terrible lens, the barely visible became gigantic: rats bearing plague; herrings shifting their spawning ground, enriching one seaboard, bankrupting another; deforestation and malarial flies weakening mighty Rome. In contrast, school texts shoved grandiose phrases at me that usually proved at best disappointing: 'Christian Europe', 'United Italy', 'United Germany', 'Abolition of Slavery'. The last, in particular, proved vilely complacent: in 1968, for example, the Anti-Slavery Society reported slavery existing in some thirty countries, while in 1991 Brazilian church and government officials disclosed thousands of slaves, men, women, children working in chains fifteen hours daily. In 1995 similar revelations emerged from China, Sudan, the Gulf; and the next year the BBC broadcast accusations of 20 million 'indebted ones' in Pakistan, including 8 million children.

School histories excluded poetry. Rummaging unmethodically, I chanced upon Chesterton's 'Ballad of the White Horse' (1911) which fused myth, legend, history in the figure of King Alfred. I declaimed silently the passage where the outcast leader pleads for support and is rebuffed:

> Come not to me, King Alfred,
> Save always for the ale.
> Why should my harmless hinds be slain
> Because the war chiefs cry once again,
> And in all fights we fail?
>
> Your scalds still thunder and prophesy
> That crown that never comes;
> Friend, I will watch the certain things,
> Swine, and slow moons like silver rings
> And the ripening of the plums.

The past was a mass of gaps awaiting imagination to fill them. I was allured by the Dark Age poem 'The Lay of the Spear':

> All is sinister to see,
> A cloud of blood moves across the sky,
> Air is red with men's blood
> As battle-women chant their song.

I repeated the doomed Caesar's words, in Masefield's poem evoking a warning from Pompey's ghost:

> The house is falling,
> The beaten men come into their own.

Macaulay and Burckhardt had been excited by poetry to study history; and for me history was neither a task nor morality tale but poetry, sometimes clear, often muddied, leaving spaces where imagination could paddle, while speculating, amused or angry. Aimed at the future, at me personally, history was omnipresent, flamboyant as Henry VIII's codpiece, subtle as Charles II's face, strange as genius, elusive as a Jacobean ghost and still the detective story packed with secrets.

I could be in a trance of beaten men, furious serfs, a solitary coach lumbering under moonlit peaks and containing a fugitive pretender. More misunderstandings reconciled past with present: a chapter heading, 'Louis Napoleon flees from Ham', was understandable in the glum light of school meals. When a farmer told me his Lincoln Red cattle descended from Viking herds, I was more stirred than by all the glories of empire. I did not, however, neglect the present and assiduously studied John Gunther's *Inside Europe* from 1936. I still have a copy, the '33rd Impression' and, opening it, read: 'Nor has Stalin the hard, insensitive ruthlessness which Slavs so often display. He has stood forward as defender of the people's rights, the champion of men as men.'

Travelling in holiday cricket teams, I found no place without its dead hero, antique ritual, dim legend, pub talk of outrage or long-gone scandal, lives blighted by the First World War, itself sometimes welcomed as an escape from harsh farmers or nagging homes. Again, I felt myself part of history when, for Chalfont St Giles, I held a one-handed running catch and was praised by an elderly gentleman, J.T. Hearne, who in W.G. Grace's day had done the hat-trick against Australia.

Youthful imagination is restless. Barely articulate, without intimates, I had to watch, listen more intently, awaiting what might never come. I discovered that dictionaries explained not only the meanings of words but their derivations. Words could be deeper than pools. I was enthralled by 'capital' originating in 'Caput Aulis', the severed head of Aulis interred beneath the Capitoline Hill, Rome, and always bleeding. Who was Aulis? I must probe further. Did the Tower of London, Westminster Abbey, conceal such a head? Gazing at the immemorial beggars always loitering outside, I sensed that, symbolically, they did.

Such discoveries, whether or not true, were almost physical in their impact, like a fuller understanding of 'listening to the silence', which transported me, shuddering but delighted, to a haunted grange, murderer's hide-out, astrologer's waiting room. On a northern moor, a solitary boulder in its silence spoke louder than Mussolini.

At school, the most studied historian was G.M. Trevelyan, forty years later reviled by G.R. Elton as insulting the intelligence. He thought history was both art and science and certainly, like science, like gardening, it has no full stops. Judgements are never final. I have seen challenging revaluations not only of Trevelyan but of Churchill, Roosevelt, the Nuremburg Trials, responsibility for the Holocaust, witless denial of the Holocaust itself...

Doubt everything, Rosa Luxemburg advised. David's heroic painting of Napoleon braving the Alps on a white horse lost some majesty when I learnt that he actually did so on a mule. This morning I read that, while generations have believed the Elgin marbles to illustrate a sedate procession honouring Athene, an unproven theory now suggests that the frieze depicts King Erechtheus sacrificing his three virgin daughters on orders from the Delphic Oracle. For years my image of Henry IV was that displayed in the National Portrait Gallery, but now the Chief Curator, Robin Gibson, maintains that this actually shows Charles VI of France.

Each day offered me more clues. London was a historical gallery: Essex Street, Hatton Garden, Crooked Billet Street. Weavers Street apparently commemorated immigrant Huguenots, whom I first imagined as Huge Imaginaries or Huge Noses. The Brazen Head pub near Paddington recalled Roger Bacon, credited with fashioning a brass head which hung in Oxford, giving oracular messages. Even a sentimental ballad, chorused from bandstands, mooed on the London National wireless programme, could open like a shutter on to a reality altogether different. 'Loch Lomond' had puzzled me: I had assumed that one lover was addressing another, neglecting the easy option of travelling together. A quarrel? Some threat? I then read of the Celtic notion that death abroad compels the spirit to return to its birthplace by a subterranean path, the Low Road. The High Road was reserved for those dying on home ground. In the song two Jacobite rebels were imprisoned in England after Culloden. One was to be hanged, the other to be freed, to take the High Road to Scotland. The body plods slowly, the spirit flees swiftly. Here was one of those matters which Lord Bryce called 'things not to be found in school books'.

Certainly not found there was information from Victor Hugo's *The Laughing Man*, from which I expected, wrongly, a succession of jokes. Almost at once I read:

> In China from time immemorial they have possessed a particular refinement of industry and art, the art of moulding a live man. They take a child, aged two or three, place him in a porcelain vase, more or less grotesque, made without the top and bottom, to allow room for hands and feet. By day, this is set upright, by night it is laid flat to allow the child sleep. He then thickens without growing taller, filling up with his compressed flesh and distorted bones the curves of the vase. This development continues many years. After a certain time the form becomes irreparable. When they consider it completed, the monster perfected, they smash the vase. The child emerges and, behold, a man in the shape of a mug.

But why? I could not believe this was literally true yet felt it symbolized something nameless, an unpredictable shape lurking within us, beyond my everyday fears, hinted at in German folk tales and adults standing together like conspirators. The Chinese mug joined the Cretan minotaur, the mating of centaurs, the howls from Hitler's Reich.

Truths were unravelling. I had assumed that schools, scholarship, art existed to improve people, but history often suggested the reverse. Beautiful feelings, Gide summarized, make bad art. People were not all of a piece. Cesare Borgia, cruel and unscrupulous, was highly educated, while Rodrigo Borgia, the criminal Pope Alexander VI, had charm, culture, sensitivity. Tiptoft, Earl of Worcester, aptly named 'the Butcher', collected one of the finest libraries in England and demanded to be beheaded with three strokes to honour the Trinity. Conversely, Oliver Cromwell, impugned as a killjoy Puritan, loved football and music, owned racehorses, allowed the return of the Jews after their expulsion in 1274, encouraged tree-planting, envisaged a national university.

From H.G. Wells, from historical atlases and architectural hints I began discerning world movement, sometimes with a foreboding that the British Empire, a reassuring red global smear, might shrivel, be guttered in the dregs of the universe. Ice ages had had their say: Assyria, Babylon, Persia, Parthia, Scythia had swelled, sagged, gone. Lithuania had once held an immense empire; the eighteenth-century Danish fleet was second only to the English; in 1500 Portugal had been the wealthiest European state. While the pace seemed dizzy, this could be deceptive: Nazi Germany had medieval roots; Irish hatred between north and south had preceded the Anglo-Norman confiscations; the unprecedented seldom occurred.

The squat brown sixpenny volumes of the Rationalist Press – Voltaire, Wells, Llewellyn Powys, Winwood Reade, Russell – emphasized genetics, mineral deposits, climate, class, tides, but I never lost my fascination with exceptions, awkward squads, the enormous comics. I was beguiled by Caligula chatting to the sea; Victor Lustig, the trickster, twice negotiating the sale of the Eiffel Tower for scrap. The thirteenth-century ruler of Castile, Alfonso the Wise, composed four hundred odes to the Virgin Mary; a landgrave of Hesse, with two fingers on the piano, wrote 52,365 marches. Much abused for extravagance, Napoleon III had his socks darned, for 25 centimes a hole. These tiny mementoes linked academic history with the surges of common life. In 1932 Maynard Keynes told Julian Bell that Marxism was merely a misunderstanding of Ricardo.

Saints possessed attributes unmentioned in chapel: St Bernard established the Inquisition, St Vladimir was a shrewd ruffian, and Saints Perpetual and Felicia derived only from the Roman greeting *perpetua felicitae*. Stories of British saints, Hilda, Wilfrid, Dunstan, suggested sainthood as a technique for getting one's own way undisputed. I later admired Petrarch for writing a book entitled *On His Own Ignorance and That of Others*.

I discovered, too, that when Hitler invaded Poland the League of Nations was debating the standardization of level-crossings. Hitler's secretary Gerda Christian has disclosed that at his last meal the talk concerned dogs mating and the French currently using grease from the Paris sewers to manufacture lipstick. Gladstone, after dining with Victoria, informed his wife: 'She drank her claret strengthened, I should have thought spoiled, with whisky.'

The 2nd Duke of Buckingham, son of the Favourite, remarked that we must periodically water our life if we wish it to grow. My own life has been watered by endlessly, sometimes unwillingly, discarding opinions, revising convictions, discovering alternatives. History taught me the way, by refuting the superficial, revealing paradoxes, allowing me second thoughts. While the magnitude of the Empire could disguise the inorganic and weak, I often found clues in small countries overshadowed by Great Powers. Like Wales, for example, Iceland had a medieval literature comparable to any in the world. I once saw a book lying open as if accidentally, but actually left for me by a crafty and understanding master, from whom I realized that a teacher can be the most persuasive by keeping silent. I read, much moved, only half-understanding, in *Asgard and the Gods*:

> Then the Asas all went to their lofty seats,
> The most holy gods deliberated on this,
> Who would form the chief of the Dvergues,
> From the blood of Brimer, from the thighs of the livid giant.

I was stirred by Auden's line about the site of an Icelandic church 'where a bishop was put in a bag' and learnt that Iceland and Viking Isle of Man possessed the oldest of elected parliaments. Another lover of the north, Philip Toynbee, a close friend, wrote in *A Learned City* in 1966:

> Honour Iceland, where each farmer was king of his own kin,
> A world where honour was paid to each rank and every calling,
> A world where no man was to another a gibbering animal.

I lived to honour small communities: a village, tennis club, school, household, salon, without rank or class rules or fashion, of solid relationships, good talk, a sort of love.

I once contemplated writing a study of creative beliefs and civilized behaviour effected by the small and independent communities: Moravian Brothers settlements and Danish Folk High Schools, prospecting all-round education, fusing literature and ecology, science and art, civics and sport. Denmark, after all, defended her Jews against Himmler and Eichmann, while France did not; and Lichtenstein shamed Britain in 1945, when Prince Franz Josef II and his premier, Alexander Frick, refused to surrender several hundred anti-Stalinists, including the Romanov heir, to the Red Army. 'Ours,' Frick declared, 'is a small community, but it is one governed by laws.' Author of *The Victims of Yalta*, Nikolai Tolstoy, summarized: 'So it was that tiny Lichtenstein with no army and a police force of eleven men did what no other European country dared.'

One of my boyhood books was Kenneth Grahame's *The Golden Age*, which mentioned a figure, sympathetic but obscure, as if seen through tissue, Marcus Aurelius. The discovery that he was a Roman Emperor led me to a book of quotations:

> Do not believe that what is difficult for you to master is humanly impossible; but if anything is humanly possible, consider it to be within reach.
> It is man's distinctive duty to love even those who have harmed him.
> A man should be on his feet, not kept on his feet.

I disputed 'Very little is required to ensure a happy life', for my desires were becoming immoderate, my greed voluptuous, my ambition boundless. I would have liked nine sisters, each incredibly rich. Nevertheless, Marcus Aurelius had maxims not very different from those I heard daily at prayers, but unencumbered with the supernatural, with magic and legend. I remain puzzled that his stoic personality has had so little impact in England, where the moral tradition conforms so many to his thoughts.

Like Shaw's Life Force, progress wobbled; but violence, lust, envy, were perennial:

We were a band of brothers drunk with all the passions of the world, full of lust, exultant in action. What we wanted we did not know, and what we knew we did not want. War and adventure, excitement and destruction. An indefinable surging force welled up from every part of our being and flayed us onward.

This feeling would have been recognized by ancient Mongols or Carthaginians, though written by a soldier-novelist Ernst von Salomon about the freebooting German Freikorps in 1919–21. Salomon had some part in the murder of Rathenau, gifted German-Jewish Foreign Minister, in the interests of 'National Honour'. Like Juenger, he survived Hitler. Nero would have felt at home with both, and with Goering, or at a Bologna art exhibition in 1976 where the élite watched a goat being disembowelled to electronic music. History, on evidence, had scant influence on morals and politics, and eventually I bowed to F.A. Simpson's conclusion that the gloomy fiction that it is a science has not delivered men from the folly of supposing it to be a philosophy.

In the winter of 1938, I achieved one aim in the campaign to survive, winning that scholarship to Worcester College, Oxford. I was primed to deliver a thesis to astonish the world.

Not so. Within a month at Oxford I realized I would never be a historian. My lazy neglect of foreign languages, a reliance not on patient research but on glib phrases, an inherent dislike of probing too far and a reasoned conviction that much in human affairs was inexplicable, all debarred me. Yet all was not lost. These disqualifications might be those essential for the writing of novels, even plays. *Tell our stories*. I soon departed from Oxford without a degree. I retained a nagging guilt about this until over fifty years later, when a letter arrived from the Provost of Worcester inviting me to accept an honorary fellowship. I felt myself a schoolboy unexpectedly receiving his colours after a succession of low scores.

4

NOVEL WRITING

The Novel was born with modern capitalism, it is saturated with individualism and liberalism: it is characteristically middle-class. Is the Novel tied to the fate of capitalism and the liberal view of life? Is the Novel condemned quietly to become an anomaly in the socialist climate where freedom, individualism, liberal thought and the preoccupation with individual fate are despised, discouraged, or, worse still, are painfully forgotten?

– V.S. Pritchett (1947)

M^Y first novel, *I Am the World*, 1942, like my historical ambitions, flopped. Edwin Muir was the kindest critic, writing that its imaginative promise was ruined by a sort of journalistic mysticism. My qualifications for novel writing came less from original insights and convictions than from admiration for others: Dickens, the German poet and novelist Franz Werfel, Lion Feuchtwanger, the global-minded novelist R.C. Hutchinson, the romantic Hugh Walpole, sneered at by Somerset Maugham in *Cakes and Ale*. My book, ostensibly narrating the rise of an ignorant man to power and disillusion, existed mostly in the sub-world of dream and intuition, not observation of actual people. Further inexperience hampered its credibility. I had assumed that a 'char' was a Balkan wildcat and allowed myself several pages describing a man fighting with it on a mountain peak. After publication I discovered that a char is a species of Welsh hill trout. Furthermore, the movies appeared to be destroying the solid narratives on which I had trained myself. My imagination overflowed, from much reading, small discrimination, bookish rather than truly imaginative.

> Behind the gardens was the vast mournful palace with its tapestries and pale, jewelled dukes in gilded frames, their three-cornered hats, silver and black, their dancing dwarfs and love songs. The bows and stately gestures had vanished with courts long forgotten, leaving their throne too high and sombre, a rock sprawling above yellow, salt-dry sands where men have no hearts. But somewhere their land kept its greenness and leafy knolls, the glens of late spring and waving grasses: somewhere the haunted riders leapt to the chase beneath the pallid, unheeding moon, and a glance from their wide, soft eyes changes a child to a fox. Today, however, the city was far from fluttering, enchanted forests. Everywhere were the coronation garlands, children staying up late, then sliding down sunbeams in tousled dreams: there were fairs and dancing, sugar butterflies, arcades, spice tents, theatre booths, monkeys, dogs so minute they could enter a glove, yet quite perfect. The Cathedral chimes alone were unaltered in the crimson, whirling capital. Within, the carved unsmiling knights slept, through deserted aisles came a sign from the night where the white stars rode and a green moon floated on the river.

This kind of writing continued unflagging for several hundred pages yet reached nowhere in particular, all description, without dialogue, significant confrontations, even rudimentary psychology. Publication was a set-back. For several years, though I wrote frantically, every novel was rejected, with increasing frigidity. For too long I had mistaken eloquence for literature. Yet set-backs can be disguised assets. I had to rethink, shed outside influences, enlarge whatever personal vision I possessed, recapture the freshness of *Tell our stories*. I must listen to people's speech, yet subtly alter it; leave description to movie-makers; feel atmosphere, colours, silences; capitalize on my feeling for the odd, the singular, the grotesque.

Now I am rather proud of those years of failure. I see my trail littered with the disappointments of talented friends too early overpraised by reviewers, soaring briefly into what Cyril Connolly called the slimy shallows of success, then subsiding, mostly for ever, defeated by loss of confidence, domestic needs, blighting of vision. 'I have seen,' Ezra Pound wrote, 'young men and women of the utmost ability fail because they failed to calculate the length of the journey.' I also met those who, completing a book, never ventured to offer it to a publisher, perhaps akin to certain games players, skilful, but handicapped by abstruse fears of winning. I learnt the absurdity of arrogance: with books I could follow the plot but easily mistake the theme or miss the symbols. In history, new evidence always waited, to warn or refute.

Failure was seldom total. Many among my friends became successful publishers, agents, City types, bankers. They look back on their writings as youthful delinquencies and are inclined to be over-sympathetic or patronizing to me, an old friend misled by futile strivings. So be it.

From apparent stagnation I was released as if by accident. From a stall on a Paris bridge I picked up a 1924 French edition of Maxim Gorky's *Fragments from My Diary*. Gorky had lacked formal schooling, left home early for 'the universities of life'. Life gave him various tutorials, from working as a gardener, icon painter, watchman, baker's apprentice, drink pedlar, and from voyaging through Russia as a tramp. He knew the harshness of common existence, its blind alleys, sudden treats, queer convergences. Pritchett commented that Gorky could never tame his extraordinary eye:

> It remained autonomous and unweakened, a kind of person in itself like one of those boys that lead the blind. Indeed, that is how Gorky seems to us: a powerful blind man being led by a voracious, all-seeing child . . . the work is strong as cheese and raw onion: wherever he looks, something is happening.

Fragments catered for my imagination, opened a trap-door to release many submerged images, memories, perceptions. Education means 'drawing out', rather than 'putting in', and Gorky, like my favourite teachers, did just this. He records tramps, arsonists, priests, officials, villagers, sorceresses; Blok, Chekhov, Tolstoy; murderers, the curious and exceptional: 'Finally Grishka went to Moscow, hanged

someone there and returned deeply certain of his own importance.'
'He's a very competent surgeon: asked to cut off a corn he cut off the
whole man!'

I learnt what I can only call the soul of a people, strange, spontaneous
exclamations:

> Dutch devils are small, ochre-coloured, round and shiny like balls. Their
> heads are shrivelled up like grains of pepper, their paws are long and thin
> like threads, and every finger finishes in a crimson hook. They inspire
> men with peculiar urges, in which a man can say 'You fool!' to a states-
> man, he can violate his own daughter, light a cigarette in church. Very
> terrible are the devils of clanging bells . . . but most terrible of all are the
> devils of moonlit nights.

With the insatiable appetite of Herr Carovius, Gorky listened to
chance strangers: 'One oughtn't really to smoke, quails don't like it.' He
hears a dying man murmur: 'There now, I'm ascending.' He uncovers
other people's diaries: 'A successful, that is, an unpunished, murder,
should be committed unexpectedly.' 'I will never allow myself to forget
any insult.'

A Baltic sailor asked to borrow a book. He then said:

> 'Do you know, they say that a well-educated American has invented a
> machine, marvellous and simple, just a telescope, a wheel and a handle.
> You turn the handle and you can see everything: analysis, trigonometry,
> criticism, in fact the whole significance of the world's history. The
> machine displays all this – and whistles as well.'

Once, from a concealed position, Gorky saw Tolstoy bend down on a
road and whisper to a lizard: 'Are you happy, eh? As for me, I'm not!'
Chekhov, in his garden, annoyed by vain attempts to catch a sunbeam in
his hat and place both on his head, ended by impatiently slapping the hat.

To Gorky, Tolstoy remarked: 'They all make a great fuss of me,
writing and so on. But in the end, when I die in a year or so, people
will say: "Tolstoy? Ah, that is the count who tried to make boots;

and then something curious happened to him. Is that the fellow you mean?" Tolstoy also said: 'Montaigne is common and vulgar.' Gorky reflected:

> One never tires of speculating about him, but it is exhausting to meet him often. Personally I should find it impossible to live in the same house with him, let alone in the same room. His surroundings become like a desert where everything is scorched by the sun and the sun itself is smouldering away, threatening a black and eternal night.

About Chekhov, Gorky thought it did good to recall such a man; it renewed one's energy, gave life a clear and definite meaning.

At Gorky's funeral, Gide saw Stalin's face, like that of a bloodthirsty drunk soused with vodka or, as he suggested to the American poet Frederic Prokosch, with the perfume of his inner feelings.

My own eye and ear were not extraordinary, but I began reading less, walking more, seeing and overhearing.

'Our dog's blind. She lost all her puppies and howled all night. In the morning we gave her some thick rags and she played with them, perfectly happy.'

Outside a pub, two old women chatted.

'Very cold.'

'Yes, it must be the weather.'

'Ah, it's a hard old world.'

'There you are then . . . my hand's gone to bed.'

I listened to an account of an old Jewish gentleman who would attend funerals of those who had lapsed from Judaism, so that he could utter a special prayer on their behalf.

I began to realize the uses and techniques of dialogue, thus lightening my pages, fleshing out characters, moving forward action and development. I mused over Borges' assertion that the line 'a cold wind blows from the bank of a river' is as complex as a poem by Gongora or a sentence by Joyce. My notebooks became more crowded. I realized that, in England, some eight thousand people vanished annually, without a trace; that scores, of both sexes, regularly volunteered for the post of public hangman.

By 1950 I had published four novels, receiving a £30 advance for each, the first three never earning me more. Writing an introduction to a book by somebody else can still earn me more than writing a book of my own. This has not worried me. To be published was always sufficient, slightly surprising, and one step further towards the Distant Planets. I was undeterred by an article by J.B. Priestley in 1949:

> It was no accident that the 19th Century produced so many great novelists. The soil was right then just as it is no longer right now. We no longer want the Novel as our great-grandfathers did. That's why I am sure the Novel is a decaying literary form, capable of course, of still offering us much distinguished and sensitive work, but no longer the form that absorbs some of the mightiest energies of our time.

Now published, if unread, I cared less for the mightiest energies of our time. Wyndham Lewis had asserted in 1947 that both England and Germany were finally ruined and the rest of Europe with them. He had, however, thrust some of his mighty energy into a book praising Hitler; his judgement could be disregarded. I was gathering self-confidence. With cheek, Flaubert had said, one can make one's way in the world, and surely I had more than cheek. What did others know of Herr Carovius or Jan van Leyden? I had discovered from Ludulfo Cartujano, via Rafael Sabatani – writers then masqueraded under flamboyant names – that Christ had received 5,495 lashes and that a boy, flogged by the Inquisition, had wept, not from pain but from joy at having received five strokes more. Who else, I mused, wavering between conceit and the need to bolster self-confidence, knew the medieval proverb that to love a woman is to delve into a bag of snakes in search of an eel?

I was on my fifth novel, believing, as I still do, that the form digs deeper into human consciousness and possibility than the screen, for all its marvellous resources of montage, graphic cross-references, startling visual juxtapositions and swift narration.

My books often had mundane origins, devoid of some vital flash of illumination, instant conversion, cosmic revelation. I was once at home on a cold, rainy night wondering whether to go out to a party, remembering that Priestley had listed as one of his delights that of 'Not Going'. Finally, I decided to go. At the party an attractive girl launched herself at me: 'Ah, James, I've been looking for you. It's some time since we met.'

We had never met. 'Anyway,' she refilled our glasses, her pink cheeks dimpled, her green eyes widened, she touched my arm, 'You're just what we need.' She gazed at me in wonder: 'You, James dear, will *do*.'

I looked gratified, and mentioned that I had recently changed my name to Peter. She nodded energetically and spilt some wine. 'Yes, yes, of course. Now, as you know, I'm a commissioning editor. No. I'm *the* commissioning editor. You know the firm so well that I needn't explain more. But the latest thing is this.' She surveyed the jostling, raucous crew around us with some hauteur: 'We're doing a series of titles, all beginning with D. Dukes, that sort of thing. You can't do Disasters, that's taken. Nor Ducks, 'cos nobody wants it. Otherwise, choose what you like.'

I chuckled obediently, thought of the great cricketer, K.S. Duleepsinhji, then remembered Alan Ross's fine biography of Duleep's uncle, 'Ranji', which I could scarcely rival; so, to escape further discussion, I blurted out Dictators. She giggled, muttered something and vanished. I quickly forgot the incident, but a week later a contract arrived, a fortnight later a cheque for £1,000, six months later the proofs, followed by *Dictators: A Historical Survey*.

Another publisher commissioned a book on the Celts. 'Just get on with it. You'll get the contract when Mike's back.'

I was so enthusiastic that I did not notice that no contract arrived. I rushed through primary sources, secondary sources, Dark Age poetry, saints, monasticism, legends, confiscations, Cromwellian brutality, art, emigration, outsize personalities and tall stories. Finally, I rang the publisher.

'I've finished it!'

'Finished what?'

'The Celts.'

'What Celts? Why?'

'The book you asked me to do.'

'Can't remember that, son. But send me a copy of the contract and we'll look into it.'

No contract, no book. But, unwilling to discard three hundred pages, I transmuted them to a novel, *Parsifal*, which V.S. Pritchett, never one to give friends special favours in print, chose as one of his books of the year in the *Sunday Times*.

Over the years I met many publishers: the lordly, the cunning, the generous, the blackguardly, the highly cultivated and those, by no means the least successful, who had never learnt to read. One craggy, white-bearded gentleman was almost always seen on the publishers' circuit in my early days, surveying us like a decayed mountain god. His actual status was disputed: he was reputed to be a director of Longmans, to have put money into Duckworth, to have advised André Deutsch. I knew him only as Mr Glad To Hear It, a name acquired by his invariable response to whatever was said to him. I would watch some young author waylay him:

'I say, sir, I wonder if you could spare me a moment. The point is, I'm in a bit of a hole. I've completed a novel, my mother says it's excellent, reminiscent of Galsworthy. John Galsworthy, you know. But I haven't yet found a publisher, and I'd be more than grateful if you could possibly see your way . . . You see, my wife's ill, the baby's got croup, we're behind with the rent, the dog's actually dead, and worse than all this . . .'

'Glad to hear it.'

He would pause, look over the youth's head and intone more slowly: 'Glad to hear it,' and move away.

The publishers Sampson, Low and Marston, who conducted correspondence in richly purple typescript, incautiously advertised their shortage of new fiction. My offer to supply it secured me an invitation from an editor to tea, near Hertford, to which I cycled, a thick novel in my carrier bag, my head primed with plenty more.

I sat facing her in her garden. She was angular, dried, severe, in a cloakish garment of thin yellows and pasty whites, like a diseased toe-nail. A hedge was behind me, gaudy flower beds fanned out to the bungalow, woods lay around in July peace. As a preliminary, I mentioned a roadside warning about deer.

She seemed offended. 'There are no deer.'

I hastened to outline my novel, its theme the influence of the public schools on British fascism. She appeared to listen but as if the reference to deer rankled like an accusation. Her face, eyes included, seemed set in concrete. Eventually, my self-praise dwindled and, as if from a statue of Memnon, she boomed: 'We can at least allow ourselves tea.'

She allowed more. A large fruit cake appeared. She poured tea, then, turning from me, cut me a generous hunk. Whilst she had her back to me, a deer startled me by leaning over the hedge, grubbing up my cake and vanishing in one swift motion. Swivelling round, from cutting her own piece, she gazed with incredulous disapproval at my empty plate. I was about to explain but was then reluctant to contradict her earlier statement.

She addressed me like a prosecutor. 'I think you must need some more cake.' An even larger segment was provided, and, again as she bent to readjust her chair, the deer swooped for its prey, expertly ruining my project.

Such episodes, like my books, gave little financial reward, but I had never expected anything else. I needed cash, however – Maugham defined money as the sixth sense which enables us to enjoy the others – and already had had a number of jobs, adequately paid though brief. I taught a spastic child to climb stairs at five shillings an hour; exercised dogs in parks; turned a handle at Hampstead Fair; spied for a fortune teller; taught English to foreigners; began, though did not finish, ghosting the autobiography of a female boxer.

I lectured not to university graduates but to small provincial literary groups and helped judge an *Observer* short story competition – won by Diana Athill, who later wrote some notable books. Most stories began: 'I dreamed that my husband (or wife) was dead, and then . . .' I pondered the example set by a Mr Blay, who, starting a bookshop, advertised in the *Times Literary Supplement* that he was willing to review books, though not disclosing where. Daily, for three years, books were thrust upon him by publishers, sufficient to stock his shop and leave more to sell second hand. I transformed into a novel a film script written by some Wardour Street office boy, set in the eighteenth century and crafted to display, from every available angle, the star's breasts, ample, even luxuriant implements of attack, matched only by the cannon on the battleships she frequented. I indexed a thesis by a militant feminist whom I liked, though noticing that, after a restaurant dinner devoted to the explicit enunciation of feminist principles, these evaporated when the bill arrived.

Once I had to interview on radio the historian Sir Arthur Bryant. Having prepared my questions, I was surprised when he handed me a list of his own, prepared by himself, artfully designed to announce that his new book was on the best-seller list, that he had been at Harrow and had written the best possible biography of Pepys.

The broadcast over, we invited him for a drink, but he looked slightly shocked. 'Oh no . . . no . . . Clarence House . . . the Queen Mother . . . I'm already late.' Relieved, the producer and I had our drinks, then went to a nearby pub, where the first man we saw was Sir Arthur drinking whisky. His expression was not welcoming, but then he recovered, gave a passable imitation of the Queen Mother's generalized flap of salutation, stood us whiskies and ended the evening singing bawdy First World War songs.

During a brief, idealistic period, my search for the small, organic, self-sufficing unit led me to the Adelphi Community in Essex, which possessed its own journal, with regular contributions from Rayner Heppenstall, George Orwell, Alex Comfort, D.S. Savage, Michael Roberts and my revered history master, John Hampden Jackson. For this, I hoped to write, when not digging potatoes, loving all within range and generally obeying its pacifist premises.

The warden was John Middleton Murry, called by Osbert Sitwell 'Muddleton Moral'. Our relations began badly.

'I'd like you,' Murry said, 'to give a hand clearing this patch.'

I contemplated a vast field dense with nettles. It was like the Test, obligatory in fairy-tales. I nodded. 'Right. I'll just run in and get some gloves.'

Murry looked discontented. 'That's not altogether the spirit we encourage. No gloves.'

Subsequently, some elderly refugees assembled in the library for

Murry's lecture on 'The True Nature of Modern Love'. He spoke earnestly, eloquently and at some length, then abruptly vanished. Afterwards an old lady plucked my arm. Would I do her a very great favour? 'The good gentleman has spoken so very generously, it's a wicked, wicked world and we are so seldom allowed anything so wise. Could you persuade Mr Murry to come back and let us thank him. All I myself want is to touch his hand. No more. Just to touch his hand.'

I found Murry reading a book. 'Ah, Murry. Just one thing more. Madame Weiss liked your speech. She says that in a wicked, wicked world we are so seldom allowed anything so wise. All she wants is for you to go back and let her touch your hand.'

I had not, hitherto, seen a man more infuriated. 'Damn Madame Weiss and all the rest. Surely they can see how much this sort of thing takes it out of me! Heavens above, I don't even get paid!'

Nevertheless, I was unexpectedly affected by Murry's last book, *Love, Freedom and Society* (1957), a study of Albert Schweitzer and D.H. Lawrence, together, of course, with Murry himself, as people haunted by Jesus, agreeing that love was essential to humanity but unable to accept his divinity. This impelled me to read Lawrence's powerful 1929 story 'The Man Who Died', in which Jesus, recanting his divine pretentions, descends from the Cross, and then Schweitzer's 1906 *Quest for the Historical Jesus*. Here, too, Jesus was relieved of the miraculous, Schweitzer further maintaining that the Sermon on the Mount was not idealistic day-dreaming but a practical survival kit with which to confront Jesus' own prophecy of the imminent end of the world. One paragraph I heavily underlined.

Jesus believed in the coming of the Kingdom of a God of Love, and believed that he was chosen to bring it to pass. Through his spiritual experience he intuited or imagined an almighty God of Love. The tragedy was that he died to prove it, and was mistaken. His abiding existence in the spiritual experience of those who had loved him created the legend that he was risen from a grave in his physical body. But Paul's account, which is the only first-hand evidence we have, makes it clear that the risen Jesus was a spiritual body, apprehended by spiritual experience, not essentially different from that which anyone who faith-fully contemplates the tragedy of Jesus may renew today.

The Kingdom was to be preceded by a Time of Troubles, for which people must prepare themselves by following Christ's selflessness, thus tapping a spiritual energy, reaching 'Salvation', illumination through dedication. Only last year I read that 'Deliver us from evil' is more accurately translated, 'Protect us from the Troubles, or the Ordeal.'

I was always very aware of Schweitzer, leonine presence in his African jungle, playing Bach to uncomprehending ears, ministering to the sick in his archaic hospital scorned by Paris-trained young Africans. He had long been detached from the spirit of the age, though, as Walter Scott had observed, this can be a lying spirit. Neither imperialists nor anti-imperialists were praising him. Schweitzer had arraigned colonialism for corrupting African society and self-respect through drugs, drink, bad faith and mineral theft and unconcern for traditional beliefs. Yet he did not revere the African, and his reports disconcerted my liberal friends. He had seen laziness, irresponsibility, cruelty, obstructive tribalism, dangerous ignorance. Of coastal West Africa he wrote:

> There are men who are possessed by the delusion that they are leopards, and therefore must kill men and when they are out to do this, they try to behave altogether like leopards. They go on all fours, fastening on their hands and feet real leopards' claws, so as to leave behind them a spoor like that of a leopard, and when they catch a victim, they sever his carotid artery as leopards do.

Teaching jobs in the private sector were still easily, notoriously available, even to the drunk, the cretinous, the criminal, and it was here that I earned my most regular income, met my future wife, established lasting friendships. I had a streak of didacticism which discoloured my novels. I enjoyed sharing my own discoveries. I liked the young, crammed with vigour, curiosity, sex. One asset I possessed was one that older teachers seemed anxious to discard, an almost total recall of my childhood, the captious tyrants, ludicrous saviours, odd sights so strangely visible only to myself. The green dressing gown that suddenly flared into a giant, the tree which without warning shrieked on a windless day, the gap in the road that led to hell.

Earning hard cash without hardship, I moved from school to school at a pace my seniors thought disgraceful, a variation on the Wodehouse character leaping from wife to wife like the chamois between mountain peaks. More pretentiously, I was obeying an injunction of Rilke's: 'Lingering, even with intimate things, is not permitted.'

The leading sins of teachers I rated as earnestness, sarcasm, predictability, conceit and unrestrained libido. I strove to avoid these, enjoying my days, and considered writing a study of the teachers, particularly headmasters, I had experienced. Wodehouse, again, was correct in declaring that headmasters are of two types, the Stay-putters and the Runners Up to Town. The latter predominated. My first specimen would usually begin the morning with: 'Ah, P.V., I see I have to run up to Town. That means I must ask you . . .' To get an audience with him sometimes necessitated accosting him at the nearest station. He always addressed his staff by their initials, perhaps to sustain the morale of those usually disconsolate, penurious and futureless. Exercising the British flair for divide-and-rule, he sometimes suspected danger: 'Ah, P.V., I happened to see B.G.W. talking to R.T.S.N. after prayers. I don't suppose you were near enough to . . .'

This potentate steered his school on to the rocks, with stately lack of fuss, though it made inroads into the claims of the prospectus: 'We encourage aptitudes for adjustment to the needs of social, religious and business life.' Another headmaster was an Anglican canon, whose scripture lessons were spirited if unorthodox. 'The Second Coming. Actually it's already happened. Not far from Bath, quite a time ago. Very few noticed.' He liked explaining that the disciples were a vulgar lot, that the feeding of the five thousand was indeed a miracle, inducing Jews to share their food with others. 'Jesus,' he assured bemused classes, 'might not have made a good schoolmaster. He had favourites, reckoned this was the secret of his own form of success. Some of you wouldn't have much liked him.' He also had a theory that the man in the parable, rebuked for burying his talent in the ground, would have been an alchemist, holding that coins could breed in certain mineralled soils if accompanied by correct formulae and incantations, which Jesus should have known. He – the headmaster – once mistook his wife for a table and drenched her with a jugful of lemonade.

Eccentricity was seldom restrained by convention or even decorum. One headmaster's wife, known unofficially as the North West Passage, always feigned deafness: this encouraged careless talk amongst boys and novice masters, often mutinous, which she then reported to B.W.C. – Big White Chief. All headmasters had reservations about my cricket umpiring: to preserve the sporting chance, I always disallowed the first appeal, granted the second. This had the useful result of giving me a Saturday half-holiday, freed from the burden of matches. One job I lost in circumstances unusual, perhaps unique. The headmaster had a tiresome boast of his descent from a seventeenth-century Edward Franklin, whom he regarded as a major philosopher. Finally exasperated, with youthful tactlessness I had to inform him that this Franklin once announced from the pulpit that his brother was God, his son was Christ and his friend or patron, Lady Dyer, was the Holy Ghost.

Assistant masters, gentlemen-rankers, habitually wore expressions often used in anti-war movies by those condemned to be shot: resigned, gently humorous, slightly stupefied or abject. Some, desperate for love, tuned in for Saturday night radio variety programmes to gather jokes for Monday classes; they boasted imaginary war records, chewed blotting paper soaked with whisky, sang in Latin but could not speak it, taught French without understanding it, stole from the chapel collecting-box, seduced maids and, covered rather than dressed in shabby sports coats and grimy flannels, competed for extra coaching jobs for backward pupils, sometimes insisting that these were more backward than they really were. Profits, of course, were shared with the headmaster. I remember them all with affection. Neville, renegade Wykehamist, known as T.D. (Turkish Delight) who so hated his subject, Classics, that he taught it with a deadliness calculated to infect the pupils: 'Another little bastard's given up Greek,' he would declare, gleefully marching himself into unemployment. He strenuously maintained that England's greatest product was J.S. Mill's *On Liberty* (1865). Also 'Knocky', who had, as he put it, been jailed in McCarthy's America, which won him respect, drinks, even glamour. The claim was literally true, in that he had been convicted in Montana for smuggling a boy across the state boundary, and his glamour did not survive a hurried mid-week flight to Amsterdam.

For a novelist none of this was useless, and I wrote two school novels: one, cheerfully insouciant, was set in thirties England; the other, *The Game and the Ground*, from 1955, sombre and more ambitious, took place in Germany during the immediate aftermath of the Third Reich. It derived not from reports of atrocities but from forgotten urges and memories provoked by unexpectedly seeing a large gateway, pillared, crested, before a long drive ending in an empty field.

As a teacher, I was actually the pupil. I realized again the fickleness of popularity, the inconsistency of personality, motive, behaviour. People could back losers precisely because they were losers. Exams, degrees, classifications, were often less important than luck, accident and, indeed, favouritism. What bit of individual personality would be uppermost on any particular occasion was usually unpredictable. Dostoevsky puts it well, in *The Brothers Karamazov*, when Lisa tells Alyosha that she has read of a child, mutilated by a Jew, then crucified, dying in agony. She is horrified but fascinated, imagines herself as the executioner, simultaneously sobbing for the child, and 'always the thought of pineapple compote haunted me.' I had no method, only my moods; I pocketed a remark of Gandhi's, slightly amending it: 'At the time of teaching I never think of what I have said before. My aim is not to be consistent with my previous statement, but to be consistent with truth as it may present itself at a given moment.' I remember that SS and Gestapo brutes had often passed the exams, collected the marks.

The more theories I read, the more I distrusted Theory. One book eulogized a Soviet school, with its habit of giving an infant a brick slightly too heavy for it, thus needing help from another, their co-operation ensuring mutual respect, love, even dedication to the school, the party, the state. It sounded plausible, but, decades later, in Minsk, I recalled this to an elderly teacher, who indeed remembered the practice, but she herself had discarded it because of the quarrels it provoked.

One incident gave me a minor theme for my 1963 historical novel *The Friends of God*. An Old Boy, professional traveller, grandly presented the school with a stuffed hippo's foot: squat, hairy, greyish. At first it was treasured, though younger boys were reported having unpleasant animal dreams; then it became familiar as pudding and finally a nuisance. A boy buried it in the garden; but the next year a strange, bright red plant appeared above it, and the dreams began again.

Looking back now, I realize that education does not wholly depend on the size of the classes, huge subsidies, dry ceilings, glittering equipment, though I found many equivalents of the headmaster in Wells' *Kipps*, with his high-sounding but bogus degrees and wretched school where 'in a glass cupboard in the passage were several shillings worth of test tubes and chemicals, a tripod, a glass retort, and a damaged bunsen burner, manifesting that the "scientific laboratory" mentioned in the prospectus was no idle boast. The prospectus, which was in dignified but incorrect English . . .'

The last words link up with an apology issued in 1996 by the Office of Standards in Education for an ungrammatical report on pupils' literacy. The inspector's prose was choice:

> The teaching is predominantly satisfactory but there are weaknesses . . . the pupils work is carefully and regularly marked . . . errors occur within individuals work . . . visits by dance and drama extends pupils cultural development . . . aims and objective are conveyed to understood by pupils. Expectations of pupils is too low and pupils sufficiently to develop essential skills.

I was still young enough to retain energy for both writing and earning a living. By the fifties I had a routine of writing contemporary and historical novels simultaneously, a useful device against writer's block. When temporarily obstructed in one form, I could move down the table and re-enter the fifteenth century. Though published, my novels of this period found few readers. No writer, however, can be certain that he has totally missed the target. Wells had written that some book, selected at random, may make a student alter his perspective, a teacher shift his emphasis, a lonely reader seek for more.

I was only slowly realizing that the novel had not been finalized by James, Conrad, Wells, R.C. Hutchinson and that the historical narrative line of Feuchtwanger, Jack Lindsay, Naomi Mitchison could be melted into the 'mythic novel', transcending barriers of chronology, realism, daytime logic. Through the limitless range of myth I could cross all boundaries and free a Lancelot, Robin Hood, Parsifal, and indeed myself, to move through pre-Christian forests to chat with Himmler or Krupp.

My seventh novel, *The Game and the Ground*, was my best to date, based upon the primitive fears, superstitions, myths, clinking about in the minds even of expensively educated children and brought to the fore by national catastrophe. Reviewers compared it, inevitably to my detriment, to *Lord of the Flies* – irritatingly, because, though published a few months after that compact masterpiece, it, too, had taken some years to find a publisher. I still occasionally meet someone who casually remarks: 'You wrote a book, didn't you? Yes, I remember . . . people said you imitated Golding. Well, these things happen.'

What had been happening was that, teaching in London, I had at last begun meeting other writers, through friends who entertained frequently and generously in what were virtual salons. The first of these was the Hampstead home of Rudi Nassauer and Bernice Rubens. Now a versatile and original novelist, Bernice was then more concerned with her children and movie-making but, like Rudi, delighted in exceptions to any rule. I well remember Rudi's slow, ambiguous smile, then sudden laughter, almost a hoot, as he gave an unexpected answer, challenging, at times insolent, to a commonplace question.

As a Jewish boy in Frankfurt, Rudi had known Nazi threats and insults. At fourteen he had seen a pogrom. In 1939, as a refugee, he entered St Paul's School with barely a word of English, and he felt his education there both unhappy and unnecessary. 'I like experience to mature in me until it's ready for some use.' When I met him he was a wine merchant, art collector, with a book of poems published, and an aspiring novelist grappling with a language which, in print, never became quite his own. Enthusing about Rilke, about Dylan Thomas, he would read me their poems, then, pride overcoming diffidence, some of his own, through which these writers' influence passed like temporary guests.

He had known the Germany I had only imagined, a land of extremes, of beauty and cruelty, dangerous tests and riddles, dark forests and glistening castles, the cunning of dwarfs and the mystique of robber barons and warlords. His own Frankfurt was, as he wrote, 'great for its Jews and churches, where the Carmelites went into hiding from the world, where the Holy Roman Emperors were crowned amid banquets and glory, where the greatest German poet sulked away his youth'. I listened agog to his quotations from Dostoevsky, and his somewhat bovine face grinned lopsidedly, then gave a not very vigorous dissent when an admirer rated his novel *The Hooligan*, praised by George Steiner, above Dostoevsky's *The Devils*.

Though I was four years older I always felt younger, dwarfed by his memories of the lost realm from which he never seemed very far away; the love and beauty, the bone recollection of terror and betrayal:

I loved soldiers and cruelty, as did other children, bravery, food, sweets and dreams. I loved fairy-stories, sagas, my country, my father, my nanny, an ugly boy called Ralph and a pretty girl whose name was Lyddia. Then swastikas and lightning SS flashes lit up the German sky, made the air eerie with forebodings, the nights were darker than starless nights, the days brighter than a vision of great arson. I remember much rain, dark skies and clouds the colour of a pig's purple guts rotating like revolving doors, now and again throwing out a beam of brilliant blinding light on the earth, aggressively bright, and redeemed only by a splendid rainbow. The weather in my young years was dramatic, Wagnerian. I pitied animals and stones, exposed to its ruthless onslaught: to shelter in warm, snug rooms was to feel the comfort of deer and foxes hiding from cold and rain beneath thickets and shrubs out in the forests. I felt akin to these animals. I loved to watch a herd of deer race down the slopes of the moors, every nerve of their agile bodies trained on their flight. The sight of deer was in league with my fears. If only they knew, I thought, that they could be shot at any time, that hunters lay in wait for them! Shots in

the distance made me reel with grief, shots in the forest always sound
final, there's just one thud, like the word Death. At least we knew we
were being hunted, or rather I constantly imagined the sight of a thousand guns trained on me. We could beware.

We would talk, talk, his pale blue eyes always looking past me, at
something further. We knew of a prisoner who had only one book in an
incomprehensible language, which he read continually with ever-
renewed excitement. We saw novelists, ourselves, as Professors of
Alternative History, and Rudi's moral focus could disturb me. He, the
exile, maintained that the battle of Stalingrad justified the most monstrous dictatorship. 'No other force could generate such world-strength,
such human endurance.' We ridiculed T.W. Adorno's ukase that after
Auschwitz, it was barbarous, and others thought it impossible, to write
poetry. Auschwitz actually demanded more poetry, more literature,
plumbing the malleability of humanity, suggesting new concepts of
progress, demanding new politics, fresh human types. At that time,
Auschwitz itself was being used by Stalin's police as a transit camp for
captured deserters and dissidents.

Masters of the World, we pondered the futures of our contemporaries
and rivals, exchanging tales of 'the Great Man', a youth revered by Rudi
as a future winner of the Nobel Prize, commended by Elias Canetti, who
was himself to win it, and who ended, with nothing published, as a
Cumbrian beachcomber. Oddly, in many country towns I found second-
hand books inscribed with his name: *The Pisan Cantos*, *The Death of
Virgil*, *Lotte in Weimar*, and many more.

Both Rudi and I meditated writing novels about the wartime resistance and were surprised to find that the name Resistance had been
appropriated by Derek Stanford and David West for a magazine
designed as 'a forum for that small body of religious independents, revolutionary humanists and rationalists with a sense of the mysterious,
united against the tides of materialism'. I suggested to the Great Man
that he might deign them a piece, but he frowned, explaining that he was
not religious, independent, revolutionary or rationalist, that he despised
mystery and valued materialism much as he did anti-materialism.

Having found a publisher, Peter Owen, for *The Hooligan*, only with considerable effort, Rudi then found its critical reception almost reaching his own estimation. Iris Murdoch considered it had great power and beauty, the moral passion of Nietzsche and Dostoevsky; Canetti found in it literature's first true presentation of a Nazi; for Angus Wilson it was a frightening and moving fable: 'the love between the oppressor and the oppressed is one of the great themes of our time.'

Sadly, it was Rudi's best novel. He published several more, coolly observant, alive with unexpected images, exotic allusions, but too often pinned to over-fabricated plots or unworthy themes and with wretched sales. His mighty European novel, *The Tower*, remained unfinished. Generous and proud, he seemed to have committed himself to some unspoken pressures which I could never really locate. Beneath an authoritative arrogance – 'Peter, I thought for a moment you were going to say that Edith Sitwell was a poet' – was someone perhaps humble and lonely, not quite in tune with us. I was never certain where the teasing stopped, or whether, indeed, it was in fact teasing. Later, his marriage broke up, and we slowly drifted apart. I spoke at his funeral in 1997 but, invited to write his obituary, found myself unable to do it. Somewhere, his talent or resolution had failed, or been distracted by his love of paintings: a complex emotional life might have engulfed him.

To Rudi and Bernice I owe much. At their Compayne Gardens home I at last felt myself part of a group, loosely bound but established: young artists, William Turnbull, Euan Uglow, Milein Cosman; writers, Colin Wilson, Emanuel Litvinoff, Arthur Boyars, Dannie Abse. Beatrice Scott had already translated Gogol and Pasternak; Hans Keller could give a chilling account of being arrested by the Gestapo; Michael Fraenkel had collaborated with Henry Miller. Canetti had known the Vienna and Paris of Babel, Hofmannsthal, Musil, Werfel, Brecht, Gide and Karl Kraus, who had said that quality journalists knew nothing and were able to express it.

Listening to Canetti, I again felt in contact with history. His massive box-like head was stuffed with memories of famous demonstrations, crises, personalities. I mentioned a novel by Werfel. Canetti shook his head: 'No, it was a poem.' I praised Stefan Zweig. 'No. He wrote for adolescents, particularly those prone to suicide.' I ventured a mention of Feuchtwanger. Canetti's silence was heavy and prolonged. Of Isaak Babel he wrote:

> Perhaps we met in a word that was never spoken between us but which keeps crossing my mind when I think about him. It is the word *Learn*. Both of us were filled with the dignity of learning. His mind and my mind had been aroused by early learning, by an immense urge for learning. However, his learning was already completely devoted to human beings; he needed no pretexts – neither the expansion of a field of knowledge nor alleged usefulness, purpose, planning, in order to learn people.

Today, I often look back at Canetti, himself now dead, the solid, smiling, courteous European and the shade of Babel, marvellous story-teller, victim of Stalin. Also, at that lost atmosphere of the Nassauer home: laughter, satirical comment, confidential talks; of people mostly young, with futures sometimes tragic but all of some consequence, save, of course, the Great Man.

One evening remains typical, a picnic by the Thames near Henley, endowed with plenty of Rudi's wine. I was avoiding one girl. She had published two books of poetry, but this did not cause my aloofness. At a previous party she announced that she must tell me a very funny story about Feliks Topolski, but she was then summoned to the telephone and, returning had either forgotten the story or was disinclined to waste it on me. Some weeks later, at a dinner, she suddenly called out that I had a funny story to tell about Topolski, and I received glances, some unfriendly, some relieved, when I was unable to tell it. A week afterwards she rang me to tell me that she was being kept awake laughing at my story about darling Feliks.

By the smooth, gliding waters were the usual writers, artists, also some youthful stage folk, exhibiting their profiles, swapping generalities.

'Bill, I do get fascinated by the ways people leave rooms. Each reveals the crucial character. I guess it's what the theatre does to me.' She spoke in wonder.

We were eating well, we were drinking better, dusk was gradually scattered in filmy patches as if at random over fields and the waters coiling out of owl country. We lay with hock and chicken, gnats hovering, fish plopping, last birds swooping, jazz from some distant hotel softly flowing with the river. Voices chattered without lasting effect.

'Oh, Arthur . . . I too believe in fairies.'

'I wasn't talking about fairies, I was talking about the Roman army. The army of Rome.'

I was soon drowsy, contented with the warm, mothy night, the moon, the tunes sliding deftly into each other. Some were singing, the words lolling and slurred. Frogs were croaking. I saw the Topolski addict wandering between groups, unsteady but purposeful, a trull scouring the battlefield eager to slit the wounded. Then a faint voice murmured: 'Did you know that Crosby, Bing Crosby, was scared of leaving a hat on a bed?'

'That's nothing very much. When we were in that village in Spain, David asked the Spanish cook about snakes. Snakes! What an idea! Unheard of! Next morning David found a snake's head in the porch, still oozing. The local chemist told us that snakes no longer existed round there, but two days later we found another head, on the steps. The chemist merely said that ants were scared of the Cathedral!'

While we lapsed into dreaminess, smudged by fumes, by hock, Rudi stood up, lumbered to the bank and silently undressed, then plunged into the water with a splash like a clarion, awaking us. Laughing off, pushing away angry escorts, some girls swiftly stripped, now one, now another, dropping white and neat into the cowled, phosphorescent Thames. Soon, almost all of us were with them, gasping, kicking, crying out, swallowing gusts of water. Very drunk, we were momentarily helpless, laughing wildly, drifting on an inexorable current, about to sink, then struggling in half-laughing panic as if in a tune, the moon glaring, the stars feverish and dilated. Youth, beauty, promise, were drugged in Ophelia waters which would perhaps deliver us all to the sea, to be strewn upon some indefinite shore, though, within instants, with a kick, a flourish, a helping hand, we were back on the grass, shivering, exhausted, suddenly embarrassed, Rudi on the outskirts, already dressed, treasuring his secretive grin.

For another thirty years my social life was dominated by the hospitality of the economist Professor William Letwin, cool, measured, courteous in all situations; his dynamic wife, the social philosopher Shirley; and their son Oliver, today a banker and MP. Here came academics, politicians, journalists, editors, critics, novelists of all ages, downwards from Erich Heller and Michael Oakeshott; an Indian general might be introduced to an authority on Russian history, the head of a Cambridge college to an LSE sociologist, a youthful academic with a future to an aged continental with an eminent past.

One might meet George Gale gazing perplexedly at Professor von Hayek, Kingsley Amis reminding Maurice Cranston that Ezra Pound was a fake, Sybille Bedford with tales of Edith Wharton, Gertrude Himmelfarb disposing of the legend of John Buchan's anti-Semitism. Keith Joseph, Minister for Education, scarcely uttering a word, could yet induce radiant conversation around him; so, rather differently, could William Sansom, who for me, with V.S. Pritchett, was the most brilliant writer of our time about London. Once, in mid-dinner, irritated by Shirley's having detached him from playing jazz on her piano so that the rest of us could go in for the meal, he methodically undressed, removing his 'planter's suit' of white duck.

My involvement with history was fortified by meeting Francesca Wilson, who had done strenuous relief work in central Europe in the aftermath of the First World War and whose close friend Countess Karolyi had been married to the last Habsburg chancellor, who in 1946 became communist Hungary's first Foreign Minister. Her book *In the Margins of Chaos* was a powerful reminder of times faded but still vibrant.

Shirley Letwin published *The Pursuit of Certainty*, studies of pragmatic rationalism exemplified by Hume, Bentham, J.S. Mill and Beatrice Webb, but I have never met anyone who less needed to pursue certainty. She had grabbed it firmly and without disposition to relinquish it. Her judgements were swift and magisterial, usually in brisk opposition to my own. My incautious praise of West Indian cricketers was imperiously dismissed; her response to my admiration for Arnold Toynbee was tart. His celebrated *A Study of History* she scorned as Prophetic Books masquerading as history, attempting to reduce the muddle of the past to neat captions: 'The riddle around Arnold Toynbee begins with the difficulty of discovery, what connection *A Study of History* has with history.'

She had trained for ballet, studied political economy under Harold Laski, whom she deprecated, and more substantially under R.H. Tawney and her close friend Oakeshott. She wrote fluently, elegantly, on education, law, freedom, morality, religion, the history of ideas, always with what *The Times* obituary termed analytical ruthlessness (a characteristic title of hers was *Against Tolerance*). Her *Anatomy of Thatcherism* shows admiration for Thatcher, who attended her crowded memorial service, without being wholly convinced that the former prime minister was the fullest representative of Thatcherism, as Shirley saw it. She considered that England itself insufficiently lived up to her own conceptions, which mingled her pungent impatience with the quieter visions of Henry James and Trollope. An England of civilized intercourse, patrician politics, traditional institutions and schools, intellectual camaraderie, great libraries and gardens, individual responsibility, a certain social decorum. Here, she could be eccentric, once assuring Bryan Magee that no real poverty existed in Victorian England save amongst the feckless; and arguing with Peregrine Worsthorne and myself that shooting might adequately reward strikers in essential services. If this sounds unpalatable, attention should focus instead on her *The Gentleman in Trollope: Individuality and Moral Conduct*, which amply displays her erudition, deep feelings and well-honed opinions. It begins, 'The gentleman has become a figure of fun' and later declares: 'The most perfect gentleman in Trollope's novels is Madame Max Goesler. She was the daughter of a humble German Jewish attorney, and her only endowments by birth were beauty and intelligence.' This book was praised by John Osborne as a classic of wisdom about the way we live now, delivered like table talk of a very high order. He cited: 'The gentleman's world does not require a choice between rebellion and submission, violence and reason, alienation and unity, certainty and apathy. It is a world full of nuances.'

Shirley, a pronounced individualist, loathed socialism, the messianic and utopian, belief in moral and cultural relativity. Gentlemanliness had, for her, nothing to do with class or income but was a state of mind, compounding stoic courage, disregard of fashion, a quiet, almost puritan insistence on truthfulness. In the *Observer* John Kenyon diagnosed her 'Gentleman' as containing 'truthfulness to himself, discrimination in choosing his line of conduct, diffidence in forcing his attitude on others, but courage in defending them when attacked'.

I never noticed diffidence in Shirley but, intellectually, and in her last illness, her courage was robust. No one was less trendy; she was almost impossible to envisage watching television, and it was totally impossible to imagine her, a trained musician, listening to screaming pop. A formidable mixture of generosity and affection and mental austerity, she was wholly uninhibited by polite necessity to praise the unpraiseworthy, the sloppy or uninformed. My own tendency towards amiable but vague generalizations was constantly chastised.

The Letwins' Sunday tennis parties submitted to the same imperious rigours. Two hours were booked, insisted on to the last second. Once a blizzard intervened: John O'Sullivan murmured, Shirley did not hear; Noël Annan moved away into outer swirls, an Oates braving all, Shirley failed to notice; Perry Worsthorne ostentatiously donned mackintosh and, seen through the gloom, what appeared to be wellingtons, to no avail. Only the prospect of the outstanding food, wine and whisky kept me at my post.

To the general tone and dialectical exhilaration of Kent Terrace I contributed little, but Shirley, Bill and Oliver were so much part of my life that I have not fully adjusted myself to Shirley's departure. I owe her much: she was stimulating, exasperating, generous, fiercely loyal.

An infrequent visitor to England, but nevertheless part of the Letwin climate, was a tall, stiff, bony figure, as if from a Bergman movie, the Reverend Dr Krister Stendahl. A former chaplain of Uppsala University, he later became Professor of New Testament Studies at Harvard, where he edited the *Theological Review*; and later still a bishop. He was the first cleric who suggested for me Christian alternatives to traditional faith: 'I happen to believe that the whole, long and glorious Christian tradition of speaking about the immortality of the soul is only a period of the Judaeo-Christian tradition, and that period may now be coming to an end.'

He would outline, with gentle tolerance, beliefs which, though not sensational, have influenced me:

The question about immortality of the soul is interesting for someone who is primarily a biblical scholar because he specializes in sixty-six so-called books that do not know of the immortality of the soul. The word occurs in two places in the New Testament; once about God 'who alone has immortality', and once in a very special setting, where it is perhaps borrowed from other people whom Paul quotes when he speaks of how the mortal nature must put on immortality. But perhaps the almost complete absence of the word 'immortality' is not really the point. The point is that the whole world which comes to us through the Bible, Old Testament and New, is not interested in the immortality of the soul. It is very clear that Abraham, Isaac and Jacob are one in believing that the only immortality that there is, is in the germ plasm, or, as they called it, 'the loins'. The only immortality that the earlier strata of the Old Testament knows about is the perpetuation through your offspring. Theirs is a view of man created of dust who is made a human being by God's energizing power, the 'spirit' being blown into the dust. That is also what Ecclesiastes speaks about in that beautiful description of ageing, which outdoes T.S. Eliot because that's what he tried to copy, which ends on the note that then the dust returns to the dust whence it came, and the spirit returns to God who gave it. Here the spirit is not the individual's little identity spirit, but the life-giving power of God, the *ruach*, the wind which is withdrawn, and so may disintegrate into dust. Dust to dust, ashes to ashes.

Krister distinguished between personal survival and the frequent New Testament references to 'Resurrection'. This latter concept expresses humanity's constant defeats and recovery in efforts to support God's struggle against evil, creation against destruction.

That is the matrix, that is the womb out of which the dream and thought, hope and prayer for the resurrection emerged out of the Jewish community in times of martyrdom and suppression. They spoke about vindication of the righteous and the martyrs. They did not affirm so much the fate of each individual. They were interested in whether God and Justice would have the last word.

'I wonder if I can do it.' Thus W. Somerset Maugham begins his story 'Salvatore'. In my estimation the story is unexceptional, slightly sentimental, almost banal. He ends it by explaining his original self-question: whether he could hold our attention by depicting a quality rare, precious and lovely. 'And in case you have not guessed what the quality was, I will tell you. Goodness, just goodness.' I remembered this on the death of another remarkable hostess, Margot Walmsley, about whom I can write no story, can only remember with love and gratitude. With Wilfrid Israel she is foremost amongst my friends for simple goodness, without smugness, conceit or cant.

Deputy editor of *Encounter*, throughout that journal's existence, Margot had full share of misfortune, though one could know her for years without realizing it. Her husband and her son, with whom I played cricket, both committed suicide. Thereafter she devoted herself to befriending and entertaining others. Ill-endowed financially, she gave regular and spirited parties, salons, in which, like the Letwins, she could reconcile all temperaments, genders, callings, generations. Through her, too, I was privileged to meet many I had admired from a distance.

Only once did I ever hear her venture a personal criticism (it was in fact so mild that, compared to what the rest of us felt, it was almost praise). A peer, famed for his sympathy towards minorities, underdogs and vicious criminals, had volunteered to drive her home after midnight from a party. At Hyde Park Corner, on a cold night, he dumped her, reminding her that she would know her way home, over two miles away, at the far end of Kensington High Street. Nevertheless her temperate reproach astonished us by its uniqueness. She gave me much; I rebuke myself for returning her so little.

5

PERSONALITIES

Remember the blackness of that flesh
Tarring the bones with a thin varnish
Belsen Theresienstadt Buchenwald where
Faces were clenched fists of prayer
Knocking at the bird-song-fretted air.
Their eyes sank jellied in their holes
Were held towards the sun like begging bowls
Their hands like rakes with fingernails of rust
Scratched for kindness from a little dust.
To many, in its beak no dove brought answer.

– Stephen Spender, 'Memento'

OCCASIONAL, very occasional offers to meet the famous always unnerved me. To be marched up to greet the likes of Patrick White or Evelyn Waugh would have risked a ludicrous snub. To encounter such people by chance, on a park bench, in a cinema queue, at a bar, though unlikely, might have been happier, though even the accidental could be hazardous. Once, at a party given by the biographer, dramatist and critic Ronald Hayman, I was irritated to see an elderly man surrounded, virtually mobbed, by attractive girls, none of whom showed even vestigial interest in myself. They gave me looks of hatred when, hearing the gist of his talk, I edged into the circle. During a pause I remarked to him that he seemed interested in Shakespeare. He gave an indefinite, slightly creaking acknowledgement. Perhaps, I continued, watched, I noted more cheerfully, with what seemed awed fascination by the harem, he had some interest in the theatre?

Save for a stifled giggle the silence was uncanny. The elderly man gazed at me with a sort of benevolent concern, then gave me a studied but conspiratorial wink, and I simultaneously realized that he was the guest of honour, about whom Ronald had that day published a biography, Sir John Gielgud. With delightful understanding, himself prone to celebrated gaffes, he then dismissed the girls and treated me to some novel and stimulating thoughts on *The Tempest*, which he had some ambition to produce as a movie.

There is, no doubt, a Book of Gaffes. Sir Isaiah Berlin, another Distant Planet, was not immune, as he related in *Personal Impressions* in 1980. In Moscow he met a Russian whose name he missed but who mentioned various writers, amongst them Lev Kassil, the author of *Shvambraniya*. Sir Isaiah mentioned that this was a poor novel; he had read it some years ago and found it dull and naïve. The Russian replied that he himself rather liked it: it was sincere and not badly written. Berlin, however, remained unconvinced. Some hours later the other volunteered to escort him to the station and finally, having warmly thanked him for many kindnesses throughout the day, Berlin requested the Russian's name. Lev Kassil.

I became friendly, intermittently close, with Philip Toynbee, literary journalist, novelist, poet, amateur theologian and – amateur, very amateur – idealist, who was to die with courage and serenity, fortified by a late but thorough acceptance of Christianity. He was one of rather too many whom I loved without very much liking. Through him, I met his father, Arnold Toynbee, Director of the Chatham House Institute of International Affairs, whose *Study of History* had so failed to enlighten Shirley Letwin. With him, however, I yet again felt I was making contact with History in person. He had been a historical adviser to the Versailles treaty-makers and had professionally attended the Munich Conference and the Paris Peace Conference in 1946. His own recollections, in talk and print, delivered with paternalistic amiability, made me feel at home in a world real, poetic and wholly beyond reach:

I remember, at the beginning of a university term during the Bosnian crisis of 1908–9, Professor L.B. Namier, then an undergraduate at Balliol, coming back from spending a vacation at his family home, just inside the

Galician frontier of Austria, and saying to us other Balliol men with (it seemed to us) a portentous air: 'Well, the Austrian army is mobilized on my father's estate and the Russian army is just across the frontier, half a mile away.'

Here was a gleam from an epoch, only a few years distant yet remote as Thebes in its heyday, of tsars and anarchists, faded telegrams and forgotten chancelleries, tropical beards and imaginative whiskers, Winter Palace balls, archducal hunting-lodges, vast hunts, docile and ambivalent crowds, helmets plumed with African profusion.

Toynbee resumes in a manner which still moves me to barely articulate nostalgia for what I never knew or knew not by direct experience but still, as it were, in my bones: 'Hiking round Greece three years later on the trail of Epaminondas and Philopoemen, and listening to the talk in village cafés, I learnt for the first time of the existence of something called the foreign policy of Sir Edward Grey.'

Lewis Namier, considered by Isaiah Berlin one of the most distinguished historians of the age, decisively influenced British historical research. He once informed Sir Isaiah that Marx was a typical Jewish half-charlatan 'with quite a good idea which he ran to death just to spite the Gentiles'. I included the following paragraph by Berlin in my 1981 anthology, *Voices from the Great War*.

When war was declared Namier volunteered for the British army. He was evidently not a perfect soldier. Some intelligent person took him out of the army and put him into the Foreign Office as adviser on Polish affairs attached to the Historical Adviser to the Foreign Office, Sir John Headlam-Morley. 'I remember,' said Namier to me, 'the day in 1918 when the Emperor Karl sued for peace. I said to Headlam-Morley: "Wait". Headlam-Morley said to Balfour: "Wait": Balfour said to Lloyd George: "Wait": Lloyd-George said to Wilson: "Wait". And while they waited, the Austro-Hungarian Empire disintegrated. I may say that I pulled it to pieces with my own hands.'

Reviewing my book, John Lehmann, to whom the Habsburg Empire of Rilke and Hofmannsthal, Kraus and Musil, Freud, Mahler and Werfel was no sink of oppression, found this a boast darkly unendearing.

Although I never addressed Ernst Juenger at any literary gathering, he once handed me a hunk of meat, doubtless assuming I was the gifted Marxist writer John Berger, for whom I was frequently mistaken, attracting such gush as: 'Oh, Mr Berger, your television lectures completely changed my conception of the moral and political realities within art.' Or, more usefully, 'Mr Berger! Allow me the honour, I should say privilege, of buying you a drink.' Watching Juenger, grey, courteous, seemingly made of iron, charged with knowledge and dangerous irony, I remembered his First World War memoir, *Storms of Steel*, admired by Hitler, and his description of the lure of conflict: 'Anything rather than stay at home, anything to make me part of the rest.' In 1998 this is still not archaic. Juenger, who survived two world wars, died in 1988 aged one hundred and two.

In contrast to Juenger, von Salomon – Freikorps officer and novelist – Henry Williamson – novelist, friend of T.E. Laurence, admirer of Hitler, author of *Tarka the Otter* – and Oswald Mosley, I admired Leonard Woolf, though on our rare accidental encounters I found him curtly chilly. He had written novels, stories, political commentaries and an outstanding autobiography. He encouraged the dispirited E.M. Forster to finish *A Passage to India*. He had been a colonial administrator but resigned from the Colonial Service in Ceylon in 1912, finally unwilling, as a foreigner, to administer alien laws and demands. In 1960 he revisited, rather uneasily, the now independent Sri Lanka. Everywhere, however, he was received with respect, even affection. Once he was greeted by a greybeard who, fifty years previously, had seen him sentencing a village headman for impinging an animal health regulation: 'Was it just? . . . I ask you, sir.' Woolf replied that it was just, and the two old men lingered together as Woolf explained his case.

In his journal Anthony Powell described Leonard Woolf as 'fantastically stingy' and rude to servants, 'because not quite a gentleman, his wife says'. Powell has added much to the pleasures of reading; Woolf did much for the huge task of helping keep people alive. Moreover, he and Virginia Woolf, at their Hogarth Press, published Gorky, Freud, Eliot's

The Waste Land, Henry Green, Katherine Mansfield. With Lord Bryce, Gilbert Murray, Lowes Dickenson, H.N. Brailsford, H.G. Wells, he had pioneered the League of Nations, Wells greedy for most of the credit. Wells had been offended when Leonard Woolf, in *The Nation*, of which he was literary editor, quoted an anonymous critic's quip that Wells was a thinker unable to think. Accosted by the furious Wells, Woolf confessed inability to remember the critic's name, implanting a rank suspicion which Wells retained for years.

The only remark I remember receiving from Leonard Woolf was: 'I am grateful to you, not for pleasure from your books but because you never offered them to the Hogarth Press.' Scarcely ingratiating, this nevertheless failed to corrode my conviction that his work and the circumstances of his marriage made him a secular saint, akin to Raoul Wallenburg, Schweitzer and Elizabeth Pilenko, the humane Russian exile who volunteered to be gassed in a Nazi camp in place of a woman and her baby. *The fight against the false and the unfair was always worth it.* Such people stood four-square, often to the death, when, to quote again from Auden's 'Voltaire at Ferney', all over Europe stood 'the horrible nurses itching to boil their children'.

My much-loved English teacher, 'Val' Rogers, had set Stephen Spender's *The Trial of a Judge* for classroom play-reading, and this, together with his long poem 'Vienna', which he never reprinted, first revealed to me a poetic link between the ideal and imagined and the brutally concrete. Spender's imagination, as much at home in Europe as in England, exposed for me secret police, firing-squads, the unemployed, as subjects for poetry, as fitting as youthful love, fire-lit blossom, mountains filling with night. I saw him as wrenching poetry from bird-filled hedges and rustic solitudes into the grey violence of streets, secluded interrogations, death in action. Here, poets were less 'songsters' than spies, resolute partisans, sacrificial victims reborn from crucial moral choices and physical courage. I chanted to myself his 'Napoleon in 1814':

> Your generals fell out of your head like hair,
> The tinsel victories became a glass
> Where all looked through onto your losses.

> The statesmen you had overthrown
> Sprouted again in their gold leaves
> And watched you shrivel back into a man.
> O your heart beat the drum out that was you.

I mused over Europe suffocated by too many medals, too much gold braid, rent by those frantic to be taken seriously; convinced that I must forego Tennyson, forget Swinburne, I told myself that Spender was the real thing.

Spender's essay on *Macbeth*, published in John Lehmann's *New Writing* (1941), directed me to look further than plot by dissecting the play into a study of time. Insisting that here the past is a prime ingredient in the present, *Macbeth* foreruns the masterworks of Joyce, Proust, Virginia Woolf, Eliot, Pound's *Cantos*, Huxley's *After Many a Summer*.

This, perhaps a critical commonplace, nevertheless made me inspect *Macbeth* from another slant, and I would now like it printed, like *The Waste Land*, as a single, uninterrupted poem. Rereading, I realized more than ever that the past, often consigned to the quaint or picturesque, should be respected, even feared, like a live rail. We might forget history, but, through genetics, the unconscious, it does not forget us. The ill-omened may have literal powers.

> Come what come may,
> Time and the hour runs through the roughest day.

Macbeth's tragedy, Spender argued, lies in his discovery that this is false. The Macbeths are fatally haunted by time: Macbeth's letters transport his wife beyond the ignorant present, so that she feels the future in the instant, but thereafter there is only inextricable bondage to triple time: before, during and after the murder. There succeeds a fourth, the most terrible, which transcends mortal measurements, becoming 'the abyss of a timeless moment', supernatural in its paralysing intensity – that instant of killing prolonging itself for ever. Ill-timed actions, furthermore, abort their enjoyment of power which swiftly becomes a wraith, a mockery of genuine authority and purpose, a monotony of self-deception and terror. The confusion of time is resolved by Malcolm, restorer of order.

I once mentioned this essay, rather shyly, to Spender, but he appeared to have forgotten it. It remains a confirmation of H.G. Wells' belief in the incalculable effect of a writer's notion, a teacher's aside.

I had met Spender during wartime fire service, which features in *A Sort of Forgetting*. J.B. Priestley had early given him worldly advice. 'Well, it's not at all a bad idea to start with a little poetry if you want to write something serious later on. Now I myself . . .'

Since the Spanish Civil War and ever-widening left-wing agitations, Spender always seemed near the centre of things, tall, glowing, sincere, impossible to overlook: on platforms, propagating *Horizon*; on radio, with reservations about Churchill's speeches; introducing a new painter; photographed and discussed, with Auden and Day-Lewis forming a secular trinity, part of a myth in which poetry could clamour for a say in how society should be organized.

Sometimes fearing that his journalistic fluency, and professional obligations, were stifling his poetry, I was eager for his *The Edge of Being* (1951). The poems in this collection were mostly elegiac and lyrical, eschewing the bluntly political, though vehement, social sympathies that still underlay his perceptions. Remembering 'Vienna', I was moved by 'Returning to Vienna', in which the poet, ageing, but after many defeats, is neither disillusioned nor despairing:

> There where our love seemed hewn like crystal
> Into a bowl where all times met
> Within the stillness created by our looking –
> There the vision of the dead seemed absolute
> Frozen within centennial architecture
> Which futures rubbed like breezes over leaves
> Lacing some lines and cherishing some gold –
> This seeming permanence was an illusion
> For what was real was transitory dust
> True to our time dust blowing into dust

> The dust a vital inward spring with power
> To shatter history-frozen visions
> And burst through cities and break down their walls.

This vital inward spring, his need for involvement, Spender never shed. In 1968 there were campus riots in America, Britain, Europe, with students demanding to set their own courses; agitating for women's rights, ethnic rights, minority rights. There were rowdy attempts by students to align themselves with the largely indifferent industrial workers. All this roused in Spender old loyalties and animosities. He was then a London University professor, and I found him happily gratified when militant rebels rushed to him for advice. Younger than him, with different loyalties, I was puzzled. The yells to eliminate unacceptable books, the shouts 'Burn, Burn, Burn', the violence even to college employees, could scarcely have appealed to his own humane sensitivity. I could not connect his erudition, his garnering of centuries of literature, with Ginsberg howling, 'There's nothing to be learnt from history any more, we're in science fiction now.' Few were less in it than Stephen. The 1968 antics were scarcely Lenin in October, only the middle-class young revolting against seniors, racial privilege, regulations, tests of talent, and often subsidized by parental allowances. Since literary excellence usually requires discipline, quiet, rigorous application and love of books, Spender's support was understandable only in terms of romantic notions of rebellious youth, though he once told me of his difficulty in refusing requests. In generous overflow of personality, he would reply to unnecessary letters, review trashy books for inconsiderable magazines, attend conferences dense with worthy intentions and with the impact of a fly falling on glycerine.

He had, however, the resilience of a survivor. A.J. Ayer thought his air of youthful naïvety concealed a sharp wit and considerable shrewdness. He did not appear to age yet, kindly, often irreverent, lacked the static proprieties of an institution. John Bayley remembered: 'His sense of absurdity was highly developed, but infinitely good-natured and never cynical. It also had the kind of wondering shrewdness characteristic of the young heroes of Germanic fairy-tale.' Deeply private in many ways, he was simultaneously the most public-spirited of writers: he and his wife Natasha were leaders in founding *Index on Censorship* in 1972 and assisting the Writers and Scholars International.

After the war, when I began seeing him fairly regularly, he was perturbed by a current disposition to over-respect scientists, in the wake of the impressively incomprehensible (to the public) atomic power strategies, cosmic research, sensational advances in medicine and quantum physics. This could obscure many scientists' moral cowardice and callous opportunism in Nazi Germany and Stalinist Russia. Stephen mentioned a socialist friend recently returned from Adenauer's Germany where, investigating some senior German scientists favoured by the Allied authorities, he had been shocked to discover their docile collaboration with criminal Nazi experiments on live people.

Never more than on the outer rim of his acquaintance, I was always very aware of him. At literary gatherings he loomed over us like a timeless sun-god, luminous, very approachable. His autobiography had appeared, absorbing me not only with his historical memories and literary experiences but with the incidental details.

Aldous Huxley, remarking that I was about the same height as himself, looked at me meditatively and said: 'You and I are the wrong height for the work we wished to do. The great creative geniuses are short and robust "pyknic" types with almost no neck to divide the nerves of the body from the centres of the brain. Balzac, Beethoven, Picasso, did not have great stooping bodies to lug around. There was no gulf to divide their minds from the immediate communication of their physical senses.'

Like much in Huxley, this sounded fresh, up to date, well researched, gently and fluently delivered and slightly suspect.

I enjoyed the story of Yeats telling Spender how he had sent his collection *The Tower* to Ezra Pound:

with a note explaining that he had not written poetry for some years; that he was writing in a new style; that if this were not an improvement on his past work, he was too old to hope to develop in another direction. For these reasons he was very anxious to know Pound's opinion of them. A day or so later he received a post-card, with written on it the one word: 'Putrid. E.P.'

For me, Spender was yet another being rooted in an international historical context: he seemed to have met all outstanding writers and artists, referring to them not boastfully but casually, as if reminding me of those with whom I too must have been familiar. 'You remember Hesse once saying . . .' 'I expect you've read Eleuysis . . .' 'Cavafy, you'll know, says somewhere . . .' He had known Virginia Woolf, whose work I had recently discovered and, watching the sea, was constantly alert to catch it living up to the shapes, patterns, overall design which she discerned in *The Waves*. Stephen liked and admired her but found, amongst his students, that her influence had probably been very small. He wrote in 1972 that, in Connecticut, 'I asked my students to read *The Waves*. When I next met them, the young man whom I had asked to start off the seminar, began: "I attribute the cold I have been suffering from all the week to my having to read and prepare to talk about *The Waves*."'

He had a habit of addressing me as if I had sunk to almost the lowest degree of poverty. Though never affluent, I was scarcely threatened by eviction or starvation, but Stephen would confide that he had a pair of shoes, an overcoat, a couple of shirts, that might suit me – 'I might be able to provide a mackintosh' – although he never actually produced such articles. He once said: 'The Arts Council exists for people like you.' At first, I assumed vainly that he meant youngish people of promise but soon suspected that he meant indigent but pleasant enough failures. He could be unpredictable. I once saw him approaching on a Hampstead street. He looked at me with no sign of recognition, leaving me aggrieved and despondent. Later in the week the telephone rang.

'This is Stephen. Stephen Spender. I hope you're not going to be offended. Knowing something of your circumstances, undeserved, I feel, I've gone behind your back and applied for an Arts Council grant on your behalf. You may think it rather impertinent, but still, as the request comes from me, you can be certain of getting it.'

Quite a lot of him was packed into this, and indeed quite a lot of money was soon packed into my bank account. He might have insisted that I be rewarded in cash, unwilling to believe that I had risen so far above the breadline as to possess a bank account.

One of his recollections gave me an instant fellow feeling, together with a sadness that we would never become genuine friends. He went on a walking tour with a fellow undergraduate, who looked 'unassuming but dazzling'. They trudged through landscapes flushed with April greens, reds, browns, they discussed whether unused razor-blades grew sharp or blunt; at Tintern Abbey Spender read aloud from Wordsworth. The tour was not a success, but some days later Spender wrote to his companion revealing the intensity of his feelings towards him. They agreed to meet again; when this happened, Spender heard that his feelings could in no way be reciprocated but that he should try to explain them more comprehensively. 'When I had done so, he looked at me with a dazed expression and said naïvely: "Do you know, old son, this is the first time you've ever talked to me that I haven't been completely bored."'

I usually found in Stephen Spender a teasing mixture of glamour and vulnerability, self-mockery and something akin to conceit or complacency I could never precisely define. In 1956 I said something indignant but commonplace about the Russian invasion of Hungary. Stephen looked grave: 'Yes. There's no country in Europe which more seriously regards my poetry.' From anyone else it would have been intolerable, but from Stephen it was mysteriously excusable, an honest, even innocent expression of a quality that still eludes me.

At Oxford I had attended lectures by A.L. Rowse, although we never met and I remember only a strident shirt and a few causticisms against the Chamberlain government. Years later, books of his were periodically sent me to review. Each review elicited a prompt postcard from A.L. varying between, 'Who do you think you are? A third-rate writer in a second-rate journal . . .' to 'Very perceptive for once. But have you read . . .?' Finally, following my enthusiasm for *A Man of the Thirties*, I received 'Isn't it time we buried the hatchet . . .' together with an invitation to visit him at All Souls. Here he was by turns warm, touchy, vain and flattering, soliloquizing with manic energy about Nazi Germany, the uselessness of German philosophy, my cousin Robert, G.M. Trevelyan, his early benefactor Arthur Quiller-Couch, other historians – most of them 'piffle' – and 'the idiot people'. 'No one has done more for Cornwall than I have and been less appreciated . . . Since Q, only three Cornishmen have mattered: myself, Charles Causley and, of course, Raleigh Trevelyan.' Tirades, lectures, confessions, some lyrical asides, continued throughout dinner in hall. Once, between spasms, having denounced 'the so-called German resistance', he paused and a fellow guest, a bishop, leant forward. 'Dr Rowse, I think I am right in saying you knew Adam von Trott.'

Rowse gleamed, he recovered breath. 'Ah yes, my dear, I had a love-affair with him. Unconsummated. Unfortunately.'

He enjoyed declaring that D.H. Lawrence and himself were the only working-class writers of any genius and that the best thirties poetry was written not by 'Wystan's lot' but by himself. He sent me many books with severe advice or admonishment and, sometimes, astonishingly, a request to 'do what you can' for a volume of verse or stories he had written under cover of more substantial works. I deplored, resented and deeply admired him. He was, despite thousands of readers, lonely, bitter but also heroic. His parents were illiterate, discouraging his ambitions. The only book in the home was a pack of Methodist sermons. Only one Oxford scholarship was available for a Cornish boy, and he won it, permanently damaging his health through overwork. With all his prejudices, impatience, conceits, he knew what history was about: it was a form of poetry which his own verse could not match. He felt its nuances and styles, lurid pageantry and telling undercurrents, its flawed but remarkable personalities, the impact of dynasties and traditions, landscapes, painting and music, sexual conflicts and the sudden moments of vision clutched by those striving to escape 'the idiot people'.

Another acquaintance, though vivid, was brief. I was at a *Spectator* summer party, in a mood of self-indulgent well-being. I had that day published my twelfth novel; the current *Spectator*, in my pocket, had a long and encouraging review by Francis King, and I awaited a chance to mention this to some appreciative and, celebrated figure, of whom there were plenty – loud, confident, assiduously free-loading. I was in a flowery recess near the end of the garden, nearer still to the bar, alongside a large, youngish, brusque-looking man with a whisky in either hand. Our way was blocked by two giants wrapped in monologues to which neither was listening. The stranger eyed them irritably, then, with nothing better to do, turned to me.

'The usual crowd, the political, the arty, the fake. Very few of them any good. I seldom expect to find anyone worth meeting and certainly won't do so today. These mobs are simply blatant cabals.' His voice was crisp, High Table, and I wondered whether by some transmutation he was Mr Berkeley Pell.

Our glasses brimmed, the evening was sunlit, roseate, girls fluttered and preened, Cabinet ministers, peers, critics, poets maintained their status. Far away I could see that judicious, sophisticated critic Francis King. People I had long thought dead nodded and muttered, clawing each other with avid, though affected, delight.

My new associate, following each gesture, feint and dodge, as he might a battle or siege – images I derived from his expression, not wholly ill-natured but as if suspecting that this party had been designed especially to ignore dues owed to him. He referred ungraciously to 'the Homintern', 'the Arts Council mafia', 'the so-called élite, a whacking great hunk of the third rate', unimpressed by my view that minorities tend to prefer quarrelling amongst themselves to uniting against oppressors. 'Quite. No doubt. But more to the point . . . entirely to the point . . .'

The giants were now joined by several ornate women. The stranger asked me my name, and with the *Spectator* review glowing I gave it with some flourish though he appeared not to have heard me and did not ask me to repeat it. He very obviously assumed that I knew his own name, titles, achievements, and I silently addressed him not as Mr Pell but as Mr Breezy. With lecturer's aplomb, passing his glasses methodically for refills from the bar behind us, he spoke of contemporary writers, some of whom were amongst us. Golding was overrated; Anthony Powell belauded by powerful friends; Angus Wilson was past his best, Kingsley Amis – a few yards away – established only by careful management by Gollancz. The Novel needed a convulsion. 'A book now, like *The Clockwork Orange* . . . combines originality of language, theme, invention, to satisfy Young Turks, with an appeal to the more strictly literate and erudite.'

'Graham Greene?'

'I've never quite believed he much likes me.' He shook his neat, burnished head and, noticing Karl Hawker, a friend of Michael Tippett's, I tested him further by mentioning Tippett. I at once learnt that my new acquaintance's own compositions ranked high, were more accessible than the later Tippett and that a symphony was due for recording. Glancing across, with some disgust, at a literary editor, he announced that he had made his own contribution to the complex linguistics of the fading Empire.

I did not feel that he was bragging but merely twirling a rightful authority that, it seemed, was still withheld from him in some quarters. His boyish, if prefectorial friendliness, together with the drink, encouraged me to respond with a story I had recently overheard. A young couple encountered an elderly, almost blind man in the crypt of Westminster Cathedral. They had chatted with him, learnt that he had been a writer, he had known Oscar and Bosie, he had known Shaw, 'None of us cared to address him as Bernie, even then.' He then invited them to lunch at a famous restaurant. They were again fascinated by his reminiscences; Henry James meeting Rupert Brooke at Cambridge, Wells, and dear, gifted, impossible Rebecca. He had several paintings given him by Sickert and had regularly stayed with Orpen. The couple begged him to come for a few days to their cottage near Beachy Head. He came but, transplanted, soon became tedious: his allusions staled, his dead friends lost glitter, he was only a relic of a discredited, selfish era. Bored and quarrelsome, on the first misty, moonless night, they suggested a short walk. Smiling, groping his way up a steep path, he joked that, unable to see, he was the lamb being led to the slaughter. Now at ease, even playful, they led him to a few inches from the cliff edge, then glided away, leaving him trapped in darkness, an instant from death, which promptly followed.

I received a rather flattering nod: 'Yes, I could use a bit of that. It needs touching up. You may understand . . .'

I soon learnt that he revered James Joyce, and outlined, in considerable detail, his own book on that writer which had set all matters straight. 'That shop off Gower Street should have it. It's well-stocked on classics.' It would, apparently, do me no harm to study Richard Ellmann's forthcoming biography. Meanwhile, *'Finnegans Wake* is actually an easy read once you've grasped the intention and method. Too many are expecting what Joyce had no interest in giving. My book will give you all necessary clues. It's a delusion to imagine that the straight, however straight, cannot be made straighter.' The giants had now paced away, with their twittering retinue, but Mr Breezy was disinclined to join the mêlée, so I ventured Renoir's remark that a circle can be too round . . .

'Yes. Renoir . . . that son of his. I enjoyed some aspects, Laughton's performance, of his film, *The Land Is Mine*. You saw it, of course. I think he was always hankering for my address.'

A passing novelist, giving me a vague flip, evidently reminded him of something unpleasant.

'I don't advise you to try your hand at a novel. There's very little left in it now for anyone without a tie-up with a studio. Too many old nancies and young ponces still clutter the field, together with alleged wits and smart columnists who think they can create the Creator. I speak as something of a Catholic. Only genius can scatter them and re-establish the Novel proper.' He explained that a writer of any ambition needed to store 100,000 words in, I understood, six major languages and thirty-seven dialects. His manner implied that he had done so. He was as knowing and assertive as a sports correspondent, and I was gratified when, again with his boyish grin, he said, 'Well, then, here's my card . . .'

I pocketed it without inspection, for we were interrupted. A sweating, porcine face thrust between us, unknown to either of us. 'I take it that you two will be my guests for dinner, once we get out of this bloody shindy.'

Some dozen of us, all men, later assembled at a 'club' off Piccadilly, over-bright, with a hard atmosphere. A small band played coarse, nervy jazz. Around the table, apart from my new friend, I recognized only Barney Keenan, literary editor of a Catholic journal, from whom, long ago, I had received my first earnings, half a crown, for a story in the college magazine.

I was already uneasy. Our host looked expensive but disreputable, Mr Breezy was already glaring at the wine list as if detecting an error in Joycean criticism or studying a list of his detractors and, between each of the guests, had been fixed a woman, soundless and unsmiling. One of these touched my hand, like an adder. 'I'm part of the settle-up, but . . .' her eyes glinted like screws within the false lashes, 'I don't suppose you'll feel up to it.'

Relieved, I was also aggrieved by the imputation. The unremitting harshness of her expression suggested that she had been tricked into life by false promises. Like her colleagues she wore an outfit of gold tinsel, very low cut but promising nothing but evil. My misgivings nagged, relieved only by the sequence of the most expensive offers on the menu and some excellent though over-priced wine. Conversation, however, was perfunctory. Most of us were unfamiliar with everyone else; the nameless host, flanked by the least soiled of the women, muttered rather than spoke; Mr Breezy lost momentum and began to drink deep and fast. Barney, perhaps sniffing trouble, told his neighbours about Baron Bradjic who fell in love with a Hungarian countess and, after a passionate interlude, fell out of it with rather a thud. She demanded a million florins, he refused, without much finesse, though protesting he was ready to die for her. Smiling, she handed him a gold and ivory pistol, very delicately wrought; he took it but, in essence unromantic, misunderstood and shot her dead.

Faces remained fixed in polite wariness. Mr Breezy reached for a bottle, then jotted something in his notebook. The women stared straight ahead, through eyes blackly framed, like windows. I too sank into the wines, saying nothing, eating mechanically, suddenly drowsy, until roused by the sound of Mr Breezy, now invisible, stormily refusing to pay five pounds to retrieve his hat. The atmosphere had degenerated further, most tables were vacated, the band had gone, likewise our host and his female, and, behind each of us, like a concentration camp trusty, stood a brawny man with a face scarred and tight-lipped, arms folded. A waiter, all deference discarded, was asking which of us would be paying the bill.

We were all appalled. Most carried little cash, I would not have been alone in having no credit card. The moment was tense, as before execution. Then Barney Keenan rose in all pomp, his red head gleamed as if over Agincourt, the awful women shrank and dissolved, he spread his wings and soared, his voice, suddenly magisterial, dispersed cigar fumes and staleness.

'This is disgraceful. I speak as a Member of Parliament, and indeed as a Privy Councillor. I can see at a glance that this establishment is in disregard of some seventeen by-laws and three parliamentary regulations. I can also see the likelihood of my having to invoke two sections of the Law of Personal Trespass.'

The waiter hesitated, the trusties sought his lead but he dodged them. Thus encouraged, our party revived. One man introduced himself as Clerk of the House, another as a High Court judge, a third as Mayor of Westminster. I myself murmured something about 'the Ambassador's personal staff'. The place wilted and I was soon safely on the pavement, accepting Barney's invitation to go and find wholesome fare.

Only several days later did I discover Mr Breezy's card. Mr Anthony Burgess.

A composer and colonial civil servant, he had begun writing novels on hearing from doctors that he had only a year to live. Such are the ironical gifts of Hermes, lord of mischief and inventor of writing, that his wife did the dying, he himself remarrying, siring a son and many novels. He had recently been castigated by, I think, *The Yorkshire Post* for (under an assumed name) reviewing his own novel there, very favourably. To me, the procedure was sensible: only the author knows the gap between his intention and his achievement. One of his novels, *Nothing Like the Sun* (1964), I had myself reviewed. It sought to display the emotional turmoil of the youthful Shakespeare, and I considered it remarkably successful. Here was a controlled avalanche of words, sixteenth-century in its reckless dash: old words were used and juxtaposed in a new way; words totally new to me flashed across my sky: 'palliaid', 'ringocandy', 'trenchmore', 'skiddy lissit', 'sigmoid', 'dittany'.

> Pallor, the endless winter's pale, sunless
> England, white ghosts coupling in watery light.

It was a rumbustuous romp through twined hierarchies of rank, wit, ambition, obsessions with colour and language, with terrifying executions, dark visitations of pox and sweating sickness. Burgess zestfully invented extracts from Shakespeare's diaries, dreams, interior monologues, workaday life; he traced sonnets, conceits, characters from random encounters, sudden revelations, the interplay of private and public affairs, snaps of vision intense as July light. Plenty of lyrical excess and, no doubt, high-class fudge, but it engulfed me in the brutal primary hues of an age of exquisite music and shuffling silks, fly-blown middens and greedy, swollen scavenger-birds, of conspiracy and betrayal, shanties filthy as fox-holes, all spread beneath the symbol of the jewelled, pocked, unwashed moon-queen, morbid and businesslike, her breath stinking, her elaborate mirrors long painted over, to exorcize the grimaces of lost beauty.

Many years later, compiling an anthology of royalty, I wanted to quote from *Nothing Like the Sun* but desisted when informed, rather tersely, that Mr Burgess charged five pounds a word.

The hazardous paths of literary success were exhibited by Angus Wilson. From his first story in *Horizon* he was soon the most discussed writer in England, glittering as a novelist, not in the ethereal atmosphere of Bloomsbury, nor in the microscopic penetrations of the contemporary French 'New Novel' of Butor, Sarraute and Robbe-Grillet – he preferred Zola, on whom he wrote a book – but in the ample moralizing tradition of Richardson, Hogarth, Dickens, with satirical sharp-shooting at post-war Britain, still burdened with imperial values and false nostalgia. Unconcerned with extending or distorting the formal range of the novel, he wished to extend the range of the reader's mind. Applause was almost unanimous. V.S. Pritchett found no fault with his strategy, only in some of the tactics: 'In every generation one or two novelists revise the conventional picture of the English character. Mr Wilson does this.' One Wilson novel, Burgess proclaimed, was the very model of what a novel ought to be. John Carey held him a cross-grained near-genius, while Penelope Lively saluted 'possibly the greatest English novelist of the post-war years'. A few demurred. The post-modernist, B.S. Johnson, who published a book with its pages unbound so that the reader, in existential freedom, could alter its protagonists' fates at will to disprove Fate itself, thought Wilson's excellent writing and grasp of the historical moment were somewhat vitiated by the nineteenth-century narrative techniques. Anthony Powell thought Wilson's fiction unreal but his criticism good, especially his book on Kipling, though, after a meeting, wrote of him as 'an egotistical sour old thing'.

I myself preferred solid readability, even knowingness, to ephemeral experiment and, though thinking Angus's final novels tired and impoverished, much admired the earlier work. His glance could wither butterflies or restore hope. He was affectionate, fluent, amusing, slightly feline like so many of his characters; his slim, dapper personality, neat, bow-tied, somewhat theatrical, in the centre of parties, dinners, coteries. He appeared, like Spender, a guaranteed pillar of achievement and recognition: President of the Royal Society of Literature, Chairman of the Arts Council Literature Panel, in demand for international lectures and conferences, a socialite and, for all his socialism, proud that his admirers included the Queen Mother and Princess Margaret, while tirelessly campaigning for authors' rights, minorities, for homosexual law reform – he himself endured sexual blackmail. Public honours arrived: 'Our latest nancy knight', the *Daily Express* sneered. People would refer to an 'Angus Wilson character' as someone trapped in self-indulgent self-ignorance, with social braggadocio based on lost, pre-war assumptions striving for hand-outs with genteel arrogance though pretending they had earned it by privilege or stylish act of being. In her biography of Wilson, Margaret Drabble considered his stories as iconoclastic and irreverent as Osborne's plays: 'For some years now, the British had been congratulating themselves smugly on having won the war, and Angus exposed them as a nation of beggars, snobs, bullies, black marketeers and hypocrites, ill-dressed, plain, timid, and adventurous only in the pursuit of selfish ends.'

Initially, I was cautious with him, fearing his adroit eye but charmed by his apparent awareness of my work and the sheer, unforced momentum of his talk. He brimmed with extravagant, engrossing talk, as if in a single breath speaking of C.P. Snow, Alan Turing, Emerald Cunard, Hugh Walpole, Henry Green. He had read my *Observer* review of a book about the *Titanic*, a topic which, as if I had touched a switch, galvanized him into performance. Always quick-speaking, he sped into a helter-skelter, graphic soliloquy. 'Yes, yes . . . Lightoller, Lowe, Smith . . . E.J. Smith . . . has anyone written a novel about those Atlantic captains? Bennett could have done it. Ben Guggenheim in evening dress with his valet, don't let's forget the valet, though I don't know his name, preparing, in thoroughly authentic style, to drown like gentlemen, though, until then, I doubt if either had ever been quite that.' His light blue eyes deepened. Looking past me, then, as if summing up, he exclaimed: 'Lady Cosmo Duff Gordon!'

That name compressed a part of himself, not profound but vital, encasing a scandalous offshoot of that desolate horror in the North Atlantic. Sir Cosmo and Lady Duff Gordon had left the stricken liner in a lifeboat designed for forty but now occupied by only twelve. The grand pair, with the force of titles and self-possession, advised the crew against rescuing those struggling around them, very sensibly explaining the dangers of overcrowding. When the Great Unsinkable reared up for the plunge, giant boilers wrenched out with a hellish crash, all lights suddenly extinguished, darkness spreading over fifteen hundred deaths, the Lady remarked to her secretary: 'There's your beautiful nightdress gone!'

Angus, like myself, loved details, and on infrequent meetings we would swap them. The former Prime Minister Clem Attlee left just £6,700; a Paraiyan who eats beef pollutes a Brahmin at sixty-four feet; when asked in the wartime Commons, by Leo Amery, why the Black Forest had not been bombed, the Air Minister, Sir Kingsley Wood, replied that it should be remembered that this was private property, a restriction applying even to the munition works at Essen.

Despite his respect for the past, his taste was eclectic. He enjoyed Auden, J.C. Powys, Gogol, Babel, Dostoevsky, Golding and, surprising only at first thought, Priestley. Rimbaud he dismissed as arrogant nonsense. He detested John Fowles' *The Magus*, which, rather ominously, fascinated many of his students, and he increasingly had reservations about E.M. Forster, as lax in defending homosexuality. His favourites, Zola, Dostoevsky, Dickens, lacked the cosiness, even insipidity, which, he felt, had long inhibited the English novel, by ignoring evil, as against mere right and wrong, bad or maladroit behaviour, from Jane Austen to Virginia Woolf, though of her he later recanted, confessing that in *Mrs Dalloway* she had 'more than any other writer . . . helped me enlarge my craft'.

I learnt from his craft more of the pressures of internal division, social alienation, loss of confidence amongst individuals crouching within the most sterile cell of their being, unable to smash the door, itself unlocked. His novels, adding a wing, throwing out a terrace, reinforcing an arch to the many-storeyed novel inherited from Balzac, Flaubert, Zola, from Dickens and James, owed nothing to Joyce, little to Proust, much more to early family life, his obsession with animals, zoos, gardens, natural history and such books as *The Swiss Family Robinson*, influences he described in *The Wild Garden, The Craft of Writing*. As Cervantes wrote, the more it resembles the truth, the better the fiction.

I felt that, like T.S. Eliot, Graham Greene and Anthony Powell, he was professionally immune – sought by publications, widely read, secure. Very occasionally I could infer some personal vulnerability, a strain from slights that I suspected were sometimes imaginary, a tendency to hysteria, or a temptation to set up and enjoy some intense or comic situation. I remember a PEN dinner at which the guests of honour, the ambassadors of West Germany and Japan, received what I thought was inappropriately fulsome praise. Near me, Angus suddenly contorted with agitation, due, I assumed, to outraged wartime susceptibilities. The Secretary, David Carver, hurried over. 'Angus, my dear fellow, what is it? Is the food bad?'

'It's always bad. But it's not that. No.'

'Has anyone offended you?' Carver's lofty, rubicund face looked incredulous, a glance at myself and George Tabori touched with suspicion.

'No. No.'

George and I, reprieved, followed with more interest.

'So what is it, Angus?'

Angus slumped back, despairingly, his features, usually smooth and composed, now taut, crinkled, as if he were about to scream. We leant forward in alarm, before he murmured: 'I can't bear Richard Church's face.'

I inspected the untoward face of the ageing poet: spectacled, clerkish, withdrawn, it looked harmless, surely not menacing or noxious. But Angus, still breathing but unmollified, recovered only slowly, not restored by a suggestion from Guy Chapman, First World War soldier, anthologist, historian, that the face be removed by the Office of Works.

Angus was oddly sensitive to criticism. Margaret Drabble saw more clearly than I did the darker, more mysterious elements within the vivacity, authority, vanity; his morbid sensitivity to hostile reviews. She confirms that he received a letter of praise from Evelyn Waugh, never one to scatter compliments wholesale. For me, this would have been a triumph. Angus was gratified but what affected him more cuttingly was abuse from Waugh's son, Auberon. Angus's reaction was puzzling; yet he would not have been surprised by a small experience of my own. Auberon Waugh had written contemptuously of a novel of mine, and very soon a literary editor sent me a set of Waugh's own novels to write a survey of them. This was too unsubtle to be interesting, so I offered them to a second-hand bookseller, who shook his head. More worthily, I gave them to the Royal Free Hospital, where they must still be comforting the stricken and the dying.

Eventually, Angus' decline began. Accidents of illness and changing tastes began it. He had prided himself on his rapport with the young, whose respect and loyalty, as teacher and writer, he so valued. Martin Amis joined an attack on his ignorance of the latest generation, which, spellbound by science fiction, pop culture, American swagger, felt the Great Tradition to be an élitist fraud and left Zola, Dickens, Kipling unread. To his chagrin, after having been been thought so satirically, so crucially up to date, Angus was now satirized as a dated and – absurd cant word – irrelevant writer, as though themes of flawed individual exercising power, grappling with social responsibilities, sexual identities, sadistic temptations, ever cease to be pointedly relevant. He lost confidence in his contact with the wider public, felt himself rebuffed; he worried about his status, finances, deaths; had paranoiac quarrels, felt increasingly pessimistic and out of things: 'I would argue that a work-loaded middle-class Thatcherite life is the end of all liveliness, all richness, all diversity of living, and I fear we shall turn in the West into

Benthamite high producing technological workday people who, after work, watch and eat and never become alive.'

His consistent, very British rejection of utopianism, that muddled trick played by 'thinkers' upon themselves, irritated those high on drug perspectives and America. For some twenty years he endured eclipse, dwindling income, then terminal illness, while selflessly cared for by his friend Tony Garrett, helped by funds from old friends and admirers. For his publishers, Secker and Warburg, he must have made much capital; though when, during that long finale during which he published nothing, I rang them about copyright fees to my disgust the girl who answered had never heard of him. Looking back, I agree with Margaret Drabble: 'His was a brave life, which transformed pain, despair and disorder into art. He himself subscribed to the belief in the creative wound, in the grains of sand that became pearls.'

Friendships, like novels, seemed, if only superficially, to root themselves in me, by accident, against probability. In one, I must confess a gross pettiness. In 1951 I read an *Observer* review by Marghanita Laski damning my latest novel. She was not alone in her interdict, but, as vehemently as Angus Wilson, I resented its tone; its obvious unfairness smarted, and I resolved to ignore her, very ostentatiously, when we met. Unfortunately, though she lived near by, we never did meet. Even after thirty years, however, my resolution – absurdly, shamefully – persisted.

She chaired the Arts Council Literature Panel, sat on the BBC Brains Trust, defined several thousand words for an Oxford Dictionary, read a new detective novel daily and reviewed it for the *Listener*, had written a novel which had been filmed in Hollywood starring, rather incongruously, Bing Crosby. She had written on Jane Austen, mysticism and, scathingly, on those Angus Wilson characters, 'The New Poor', with their smart suits and fine addresses, complaining that socialism was robbing them of their birthright. In letters to the press she castigated the grammar and illiteracy of officials and celebrities, not least of the bestselling Daphne du Maurier. During a period of student radicalism, for a radio programme she collected a crowd of undergraduates, read them Kipling's 'If' – a homily much admired by Kaiser Wilhelm II – and invited their comments, which were often surprising. Some found it bemusing, incomprehensible, scoutmasterish; others an example of British stoicism, Victorian uplift and 'socialism in a nutshell'. I had to admit that the programme was admirably devised, impeccably managed.

One day, at a large Regent's Park gathering, a small, brisk, bright-eyed woman accosted me with the capital charge, 'Wasn't it you who wrote that extraordinarily silly little piece in the *New Statesman* about the semi-colon?'

It was not, but her manner so unnerved me that I gave a guilty nod. Unexpectedly, she smiled forgivingly, and recharged. I contrived to switch the subject to Kipling, quoting with fair accuracy a favourite maxim of his: 'All the earth is full of tales to him who listens and does not drive away the poor from his door. The poor are the best of tale-tellers, for they must lay their ear to the ground every night.'

We became good friends: she was hospitable, supportive, encouraging and, now that she is dead, I regret the more that callow pettiness, self-damaging, as it usually is.

(The worst review I ever received was not of a book, however, but of myself, from my ex-wife: 'Yes, it is true that I have cancer. I did not want to tell you as I knew you would not be interested. I have six months.' An unanswerable indictment of a marriage which lasted fifteen years.)

Another writer I avoided through the decades was Doris Lessing. Not from any adverse comments, for she would not have read me, but from awe of her accomplishments, her free-moving, interlocking spheres of intellectual, political and social inquiry. Beside her, most younger writers, however fashionable, seemed to me not knowledgeable but merely knowing.

Around 1995 I did find myself talking to her. She was friendly, unassertive, delightful. To my annoyance a youth joined us. Ignoring me, he began in full throttle:

'Miss Lessing, I cannot tell you how much I admire you . . . I absolutely loved your Balkan trilogy. It happens that I know Romania well and recognized every inch . . . your sense of balance, the war and all those personal relationships . . . Forsterian, if I may say so . . . the atmosphere, the Pringles, not a word out of place. And the sequel, it came later, of course it did . . . those masterly battle scenes, unimaginable even to those who were there, they make the war worth fighting.'

He gasped like an expiring cod. Doris Lessing had listened with detached civility, then gave me a smile, small but gracious with forbearance, humour, even a brief comradeship. I distracted the enthusiast before he could award an enconium for her marvellous concept of that visit to the lighthouse – mesmeric, enchanting, ravishing – leading to Lily Briscoe's realization that she had had her vision. Rather later, he resurfaced: 'I'm not interested in politics, only in civilization, so that you can say I represent it.' None of us actually did.

My pupils during the fifties and sixties, who delighted to teach me the facts of contemporary literature, assured me that our world had no need of President Ike, of de Gaulle or Eden, even perhaps Chairman Mao; it needed Che Guevara, of course, but perhaps more decidedly the righteous values sturdily upheld in the heroic fables of J.R.R. Tolkien. To safeguard my position I glanced at these but, so loving the original sagas, with which the young were unconcerned, I remained indifferent, despite Auden's much-trumpeted recommendation.

Tolkien, however, did me a service. I received a peremptory summons from an Income Tax satrap to attend his pleasure and explain discrepancies in my tax return that appeared unusual and, by implication, criminal. In reality, I was not criminal but slovenly; I pondered escape routes. The official's name was a scrawl, perhaps only a bunch of initials. I consulted Rudi Nassauer, who, while advising me to confer with a friend of his – very clever, very expensive – told me the official's name. Tolkien.

The rest was easy. I was soon seated in a drab office facing a narrow, sharp-featured individual whose very edges seemed frozen. I admitted the charges, heavy with contrition. 'Yes, I have been horribly careless. Inexcusable. My only excuse . . . well, I'm afraid, sir, that you'll find this unbelievable, but I can only submit that in my world, writers and so on, trivial, in places squalid, the hazards are unusual, easily overlooked from grander social concerns. The truth is . . .' – here I may have stammered slightly, possibly reddened, 'during this period I discovered a writer I hadn't then heard of . . . extraordinary as it may seem . . . but of a quality, let me not exaggerate, so stupendous that it actually left me dazed,

shaken, so that I was unable to grasp the essentials of the really important factors like politics, domestic duties, and, I have to say, taxation.
Public spirit in action.'

I had not, hitherto, ever seen such disbelief on a human face. His very
nose sneered. His words were bitten off and left unchewed: 'And what is
the name of this very remarkable man of letters?'

I was abjectly apologetic for hinting at superior knowledge. 'I am
afraid, sir, that you may not know of him. He lives far away, in Oxford,
where he's a professor, very wise, gracious, something of a cult figure,
though not exactly Miss Christie or the late Sir Arthur . . .'

'Yes, yes, but he must have a name. What is it?'

'Tolkien.'

'Tolkien!' The man really did yelp. I hastened to embellish. 'That's
correct. J.R.R. Tolkien. Professor Tolkien.'

He rose, braced himself as if for a handstand or high dive, though
instinctively I had stiffened for a hefty slap. This did not come.
Momentarily we made a tableaux of tensed executioner and quivering
victim, then he pressed a bell and, as a girl hurried in, his expression
melted into a conspiratorial grin. 'J.R.R.T. My cousin! Now, tea or coffee,
while we dispose of our little matter?'

I suspect that had I said 'brandy' he would have rushed to supply it.
My absurd statistics were swiftly, painlessly revised, and we were soon
discussing children's books, the girl joining in, further developing my
status by revealing that she had read and enjoyed one of my own, *The
Shadow Land*.

I suppose most of us feel ourselves failures, conscious of what we are
and what we had early planned to be, however fiercely we conceal our
private horizons. The most conspicuous failure I knew was the Soho
poet Paul Potts. Tall, gaunt, impoverished, he possessed no income, for
long periods no conceivable address and, though loving children, was
unimaginable with a wife, save one belonging to someone else. His gaze
was an unending search for prey: food, drink, money, publication. He
was vehement, often alarming, in defence of minorities – the oppressed,
the disliked, the shunned, the very plain, the stinking. He was a sponger,
a thief, and, in drink – he was seldom out of it – a bore. Scornful, defiant,

he was a parody of the down-at-heel but romantic Bohemian, the beloved vagabond. Eventually, barred from his cherished hunting grounds, the Soho pubs, he ended dreadfully, accidentally burning to death in a squalid room.

I could never envisage him in anything but a scarf, jacket, trousers unlikely to have been bought by himself. One hot midsummer noon, however, a barrage of hoots, blasts, horns sounded as, ignoring all traffic, a man strode across the Haymarket in a very clean, expensive, fur-tipped overcoat, aiming at me. Paul. He said nothing, nodded and, puckishly satisfied, tapped the overcoat, possessively, affectionately, then vanished back into the indignant traffic.

I much disliked him, dreaded his approach. Once, calling on me to take ten shillings, he remained three days, departing stealthily with a clutch of my books. Subsequent offers to stay with me more permanently I bought off with dane-geld, though always with some twinges of shame, having failed in common charity and respect for a fellow writer.

Against harsh odds, Paul doggedly persisted with his poems, his one full-length book, his reviews, and retained considerable affection from others. He had been befriended by Orwell, whom he called Don Quixote on a Bicycle. Women were prone to assist him, children enjoyed him as an uncle from fantasy. Derek Stanford, whose friendship with Muriel Spark may not have survived the publication of her autobiography, has written with some feeling that in profile from various angles, Potts resembled a clown, a Shakespearian tragic actor, a ruddy-faced Celtic farmer. (Stanford himself had once argued in a Westminster pub with William Joyce, 'Lord Haw Haw', subsequently hanged for treason, about artistic freedom and Hitler's suppression of 'degenerate art' which Joyce fluently defended with citations from Plato.)

Had Paul Potts been allowed royalties on the stories told of him, many of them true, he would have died rich. Here, I would like to leave in his memory a passage from his 1949 tribute to Walt Whitman:

I have tried desperately to remain restrained in writing this essay, because in whatever room I have lived in since I left my nursery, *The Leaves of Grass* has always been an inhabitant too. In these poems of his, you will see what one means when one says that the whole basis of Democracy's claims to man's attention, are the very ideas and beliefs which are crowded into these American poems.

They can say what they like about Walt Whitman. But whosoever believes and has the courage and the sense to act upon that belief, that beauty is the private property of all men and not merely the privilege of the few, will love Walt Whitman and his ferry boats, his horse-drawn trams and his yawp, his litanies, and his catalogues, his Pete Doyle and his Abraham Lincoln, his contradictions and his self-assertions, his huge hungry dreams and his few great lyrical poems that are equal to all, and are surpassed by none of the great poems of this language.

Much of what followed was also appropriate to Paul himself.

He was never a success, he had more difficulty in getting an editor to accept a poem at thirty-five than Stephen Spender did when he was twenty-five. Unlike most people who possess it, Whitman's literary greatness never protected him from the rough and tumble of the ordinary life of a person of no position and small means. He had no Ayot St Lawrence, no town house; no publisher was ever in a hurry to print him, no committees rushed to shower him with literary awards. He was always a target for the viciousness of the usual nonentities who form so large a fraction of any literary community. He was never popular with the public.

Paul added: 'Literature indeed has many great men, but he was her only great child. Walt Whitman would not have hurt a butterfly, but neither was he afraid of a bully.' Paul Potts was not a great man, but he was no bully and he was unafraid: he had many failures, but I did not think this feeling for Whitman the mark of failure.

6

GROWING UP

Always keep Ithaca fast in your mind,
To reach it is your final aim.
But be not in the least hurry.
Better let the voyage last for decades;
and even drop anchor at Ithaca in old age,
Wealthy in all you have gathered in sailing there,
not expecting that island will itself yield riches.

Ithaca has given you the beautiful journey,
Without Ithaca you would never have started.
          – C.P. Cavafy, from 'Ithaca'

An immortal soul always learning and forgetting in successive periods of existence, having seen and known all things in one time or another and by association with one thing, recovering all.

          – Plato

WE hold more than we realize; reading and writing uncover this, enlarging our potential. In my early twenties I still remained obsessed by Virginia Woolf's *The Waves*. Its fluidity, movement of words, freedom from stagy plotting, its freshness, seconded the impact of Gorky's *Fragments*. I had read nothing like it. It further, though never quite wholly, liberated me from bondage to the Old Masters – Feuchtwanger, Alfred Neumann, Bennett, Wells – and was a brilliant milestone on the road to Proust, Joyce and the German novelist Hermann Broch, author of the magisterial *The Death of Virgil*. Though later Conrad and Mann, Tolstoy and Dostoevsky were to make me conscious of her limitations, she articulated for me much that I had wordlessly sensed, during long hours of privacy and in the marvellous territories of sleep, also in Emlyn Williams' public readings of Dickens, which taught me many intimations of modernism lying undetected within his massive plots. I could grasp more tightly the gifts of hills, shore and fields – and of dinner parties and midnight talks. She enlarged the tiny, reduced the immense. Henceforward I would feel more urgently Sherlock Holmes' distinction between seeing and observing, be more distinctly aware of the flight of the white owl between moonlit trees, the light on a leaf in the wind, a woman's intent gaze, apparently at nothing. Virginia Woolf slowed up the pace of my own thoughts and reactions; I could feel new patterns within a rose, a bowl, a strip of satin; membranes of sensation often crushed by my greed for a story and easy solutions. Her breathless sensitivity was easily sneered at; but E.M. Forster, discussing *The Waves*, called it an extraordinary achievement. 'It is trembling on the edge. A little less – and it would lose its poetry. A little more – and it would be over into the abyss, and be dull and arty. It is her greatest book, though *To the Lighthouse* is my favourite.'

My collection of her books I owe not to affluence but to one more apparent accident. In small talk at dinner I mentioned that I would like to possess her complete works. Next day I did. The immense parcel was delivered, but anonymously, so that I have felt indiscriminate warmth to those eleven fellow guests, hoping indeed to one day find them regrouped so that I can murmur that I lack the complete output of Balzac.

Eventually I attempted in such novels as *Aspects of Feeling* (1986) to fuse her aestheticism and inner consciousness, the evanescent gist of being, with my own addiction to myth and ritual, the inability of sophisticates to escape the primitive, and the outwardly formal world of public issues and conflict, Forster's 'telegrams and anger', aware of the dangers of total submission to anyone, to anything. I found that, like myself, Virginia Woolf sometimes worried about her possible lack of deep feelings: 'Do I fabricate with words, loving them as I do?' My 1968 novel *The Story Teller* owed something to *Orlando*. It spread over five centuries, the same characters undergoing multiple transformations, the trickster Loki becoming a stable-boy wiseacre, court jester, cabaret clown, movie comedian. Rejected by nineteen publishers, it was accepted, courageously, doubtless unprofitably, by Peter Owen.

*

Virginia Woolf was always a Distant Planet. I had friends like Harold and Benedict Nicolson who had known her well, and I loved hearing them talk of her, but I would have been out of place at her gatherings, though I would have been glad of one, probably one only, private tea with her.

Her reputation today is equivocal. I read again Anthony Powell's *Journals* and discover that *The Waves* is 'twaddle', Woolf herself not much better: 'What a dreadful woman she was, humourless, envious, spiteful, the embodiment of all the Victorian prejudices against which she was supposed to be in revolt, hating servants and "poor people" while attending Labour Party Conferences every year.' For good measure, he found Graham Greene 'wholly unreadable' and declared that Gabriel García Márquez wrote 'rot'.

Iris Murdoch has mentioned, with implied approval, a current opinion that Woolf's novels had too much luminosity based on 'insufficient stuff'. For L.P. Hartley, Woolf was 'a crashing snob', lacking wit and humour, with a cruel though effective tongue. Wyndham Lewis in 1934 rated her 'extremely insignificant'.

Her friends, by contrast, remembered her love of fun. From childhood Nigel Nicolson recollected the humour in her voice and a faint touch of malice: 'She never varied her manner between grown-ups and children. She would talk to us as though we were her adult contemporaries and speak absolutely frankly about people whom we knew. There was always a great deal of laughter.' For him, she was the most remarkable human being he had ever known.

To Pritchett, she was 'the mistress of comedy', and I found deft humour in *Flush* and *Between the Acts* and in the style running through *The Common Reader*, where a reading of 'Dr Burney's Evening Party' would abash anyone who thought her humourless. Elizabeth Bowen, who thought her a genius, had lasting memories of her 'great whoops of laughter'. Pritchett also reckoned her a genius and warned against those who thought her a dreamer remote from waking life, effortlessly capturing butterfly superficialities or, as Q.D. Leavis put it, an 'idle social parasite'. Idle – author of over thirty books, several yards of essays, reviews, letters, and co-publisher and commissioner of some of the finest books and translations available. She assisted in a 1919 railway strike, taught at Morley College, worked for female suffrage, the Women's Co-operative Guild, her local Labour Party and Women's Institute. She admired the raucous, bawdy Marie Lloyd. Forster, furthermore, wrote of *Three Guineas* that, following her nephew's death in Spain, it was a savage indictment of war and male aggression. Pritchett continued: 'Her history of madness, the tragedies of her early life had made her familiar with terror. One may even feel that her imaginative prose has wildness in it and that her laughter, as she breaks life down into moments, is a skirmish with alarm.'

Disputes rattled on. Rebecca West dismissed *The Waves* as 'Pre-Raphaelite kitsch and should be forgotten . . . though there was something about her, which was unusually clean and unsoiled.' For Spender, the novel was a book of great beauty and a prose poem of genius:

> One is either convinced by a poetry which seems as beautiful to me – dare I say it – as *Les Illuminations*, or one has eyes that do not see, ears that do not hear. Despite Bloomsbury's irreligion, which Virginia Woolf loyally shared, *The Waves* is essentially a religious or mystical work, a poem about vision, prayer, poetry itself, the open and aware attention which people can pay to one another within the context of shared values and circumstances throughout life.

Other critics claimed a scientific slant, that *The Waves* depicted at least the atmosphere of her contemporaries, Jeans and Edington, with their theories of atoms, physics, cosmology. The critic Paul Levy compared the technique of *The Waves* and its sextet to the interplay of atoms forming molecular units in combination, dissolving and recombining them. A process akin to coeval developments in poetry, painting, the cinema, modernist criticism, physics and historical analysis.

In 1997 in the *Spectator* Philip Hensher revived an attack made by D.S. Savage forty years earlier in *The Withered Bough*, his symbol for the British novel led by Joyce, Woolf, Forster, drained of elemental juices, with talent squandered by theory, unconcern for real people and on impersonal issues:

Plenty of writers are horrible people, of course, and it's something that doesn't matter if they are good writers. But Woolf's novels must, I suppose, be responsible for putting more people off serious modern fiction than any other writer. They are truly terrible books, written in a language never spoken by any human being, and written, I suppose, only by Meredith or Elinor Glyn . . . There is never an ordinary sensation in Woolf; no one ever thinks 'that's quite a nice dress' or 'what a comfy chair.' Rather, a beef stew, a scarf, a shower of rain are routinely greeted with a ludicrously got-up ecstasy, quite false to ordinary experience and designed, not to explain anything, but to demonstrate the writer's extraordinary sensitivity.

Allowing some merit in *The Waves*, he concludes: 'But, as a whole, her awful poetic effusions are inferior to the elegant and serious work of her despised Arnold Bennett.'

Anthony Burgess was more considerate, twinning her with Joyce as richly appointed trains without engines, though perfectly inhabitable, Joyce being far more significant. E.M. Forster claimed that she pushed the light of the English language a little further against darkness. As a critic she could blunder, even remark that Russian fiction lacked comedy. But, for me, she made writing a temptation and delight.

One personal recollection which I treasure is from 1942, a dark time of war, when I listened to Forster deliver the Rede Lecture at Cambridge in memory of Virginia Woolf. That quiet, civilized voice, gently probing, affectionate but not sentimental, seemed part of the Resistance, on behalf of a culture and people, stubborn, independent, ironical, decent and brave, threatened by a barbarism which lacked even the barbaric virtues.

Her essays communicated her delight in books: she did not think literature a penance endured to tot up academic points. Leavis, despite remarkable insights, made it an argument, a brief. Forster reflected:

She liked writing with an intensity which few writers have attained or even desired. Most of them write with half an eye on their royalties, half an eye on their critics and a third half eye on improving the world, which leaves them with only half an eye for the task on which she concentrated her entire vision.

He ended: 'And sometimes it is as a row of little silver cups that I see her work gleaming. "These trophies," the inscription runs, "were won by the mind from matter, its enemy and its friend."'

Very slowly, though tenaciously, I was learning to co-ordinate themes and characters, ideas and feelings, literature and science, words and the graphic and musical arts. *To the Lighthouse* had been seen in terms of a sonata. De Chirico's paintings, Rimbaud's 'Le Bateau Ivre', Kurt Joos' *The Green Table* helped develop my casual fluency to more serious approaches. I mused over Schwitters' line, 'Blue is the colour of thy yellow hair.' Abstractions and black silences existed within noisy, jostling crowds: menacing tunnels ran beneath solemn committees. Auden wrote in 'As I Walked Out One Evening':

> And the crack in the tea-cup opens
> A lane to the land of the dead.

Flush with discoveries, in the mood of overleaping frontiers, finding hidden resemblances within opposites, I received, more or less complete, as if from what Rilke, evoking music, called the other side of the air, my novel *The Tournament*, the one most crucial to my fortunes.

I was reading Huizinga's *The Waning of the Middle Ages*, which plausibly outlines the rationale beneath much that I had hitherto thought merely grotesque, extravagant, inexplicable, perhaps meaningless and which connected with a paragraph that had excited me in Thomas Mann's *Buddenbrooks*: 'Often the outward and visible material signs and symbols . . . only show themselves when the process of decline has set in. The outer manifestations take time . . . like the light of that star up there which may in reality be already quenched when it looks to us to be showing at its brightest.' I remembered that of the three Hohenzollern kaisers the most showy and boastful was not the first but the last. Then I was arrested, as if buffeted, by one paragraph, which began by stating that in

1425 the Duke of Burgundy challenged Humphrey, Duke of Gloucester, to a duel to settle a political dispute:

> All was ready for the conflict: the magnificent armour and the state dresses, the pavilions, the standards, the banners, the armorial tabards for the heralds, everything richly ordained with the Duke's blazons and with his emblems, the flint-and-steel and the Saint Andrew's Cross. The Duke had gone in for a course of training, 'both in the abstinence in the matter of food and by taking exercise to keep him in breath.' He practised fencing every day at his park at Hesilin with the most expert masters . . . but the combat did not take place.

In those last seven words I saw, as if at a seance, an entire story as I realized what all Europe had known, that the combat had never been intended to occur. My novel was already as if outlined on a blackboard, or rather a board crimson streaked with black, for I had first envisaged it as a painting, then as a ballet, in which magnificence and formality are countered by plague and panic, decorum by love, appetite by responsibility, a momentous clash of colours against stylized Uccello patterns and street confusion, performed to the music of Dufay and Josquin.

Here, I realized, could be my best option in fiction, the exposure of the historically remote or mythical, yet fitting it into both the permanent and the contemporary, while not forgetting the random and inconsequential. Ritual changes to myth, fact to legend, history to tall stories, each with some residue of truth. All knowledge, Plato had taught, is recollection. Myth revokes time but preserves the perpetual essence. The Huizinga gift was perhaps less accidental than it appears: in ancient Greek the word for 'windfall' meant 'belonging to Hermes'.

People's perceptions are seldom unambiguous. I knew that Paris crowds assembled in 1836 for the return of Napoleon's remains for a state interment. A white horse bearing Napoleon's saddle led the ornate procession, and the awed onlookers whispered that it was the Emperor's own horse, Marengo. They knew that it could not be; simultaneously they believed it. Also, of the unicorn, Rilke had written:

This is the creature that never was,
People never knew it, nevertheless
They loved its movement, its rhythm,
Its need, its mild and serene expression.
It did not exist, yet, because they so loved it,
It became alive.

I wished one day to escape from the historical novel, stretching from Scott to Mary Renault and Alfred Duggan, Alfred Neumann and Feuchtwanger, and which I had duplicated in *Enemies*, to the mythic novel carved out so majestically in Thomas Mann's *Joseph* sequence. However, I first needed to go beyond the superficial, in snaring not the dates and facts of an age but its spirit, colours, elegies, the deviousness of its pieties and sexualities, the sheerness of its hunts and battles. I must feel, I must be, my own Duke, at the hunt, and ask questions perennial, if often unuttered, linked to Acton's precept to study not periods but problems. Everything sparkles with exceptions, the homogeneous does not exist; questions of being, violence, self-knowledge remain, usually unanswered.

The Duke swerved towards a clearing. In these swerves, in this speed, this elation of dust, sunlight, the panting, vicious dogs and the victim ahead, lurked music and the dance. Where did riding end and music begin? Speed of horses was reflected in the body; blood rushed, the spirit soared; songs abounded, though unheard. Did the stag exist, was it there, crashing ahead, or did it live only in these narrowed, transfixed faces peaked with cruel intensity. Were they hunting, or were they mysteriously in flight? The fleeting moment was now like a certain turn in battle when, for a dazzling space, you cannot decide whether you are trapped in victory or rout, but are poised in a bloody commingling of both.

Pace and mindlessness: landscape of soul; bright air above the moon.

The Tournament, republished in 1984, helped me develop those early historical readings and intimations, partially liberated me from nineteenth-century form, giving me access to regions distant but familiar, strange but recognizable. In several subsequent novels I had to recast people, subtract external manners and leave what would have been theirs in any period. In *The Tournament* I presented an intellectual and political élite moving above a superstitious, illiterate populace with which it shared more than it realized, until common crisis taught it better. Its leaders I based upon personal friends and acquaintances: Philip Toynbee, Stephen Spender, A.J. Ayer, Benedict Nicolson, my wife and myself, facing crises, temptations and anxieties common to all periods, but in far-off surroundings and circumstances, and often with intellectual premises intense and primitive.

Illiteracy was a stimulating imaginative challenge. The mind of an illiterate, like that of the blind, must have its particular nuances, shapes, tints, formations, apprehensions, responses to silence, movements, temperature. Laughter, tears, oaths, search for truth, always existed but with changing implications. I remembered how the fifteenth-century populace roared with laughter at the execution of a French nobleman; how the wise and virtuous Emperor, in Marguérite Yourcenar's *Memoirs of Hadrian*, a long novel, without dialogue, has a criminal's throat cut in his presence by a sorcerer, hoping that the soul, briefly hovering between life and death, would reveal the future. I had to ponder the effect on other imaginations of birds, shadows, boundaries, blood, planets, numbers, names. Like our children, our forebears would have been both more and less than ourselves. In solitude, in sleepless early mornings, in misery, in dream, I could relapse into a dimension where parallel lines meet, where we crouch from wolves, where astrology and clairvoyance invade presidential palaces and the boardrooms of multinationals.

Some years later I became obsessed with the colour green, startled, perhaps, by an observation of Wilde's: 'He had that curious love of green, which, in individuals, is always the sign of a subtle, artistic temperament, and in nations is said to denote a laxity, if not decadence, of morals.'

I sensed a novel looming but could only await the annunciation. A forced novel is inorganic, unfelt, too crudely manufactured – and often commercially triumphant. I, so to speak, lay back, allowing green associations to float through me, free, unorganized, until one should finally alight, shed disguise, become my book needing only to be written. In all hours I was haunted. Green was the hue of the Muslim paradise, thus both feared and glamorized throughout Christendom. Green faces lurked beneath faces on railway platforms at night, starting a Simenonesque false start. There were the Greens, Irish rebels; also the subversive Green Ribbon Club baying for Shaftesbury and the Protestant Duke. There flickered the green of Long John Silver's parrot; *The Green Table*; Rimbaud's 'Voyelles' – 'A' black, 'E' white, 'I' red, 'U' green, 'O' blue – and Lorca's 'Green, Green, how much I love you, Green.' I daydreamed of the green of expensive book-bindings, the innocence of fern, the Adams' green marble at Syon House, the thin green of a Canaletto sky, a dyed feather in a wide-brimmed Neapolitan hat, the Green Knight riding away holding his severed head, and at least one Hanoverian green wig. I read of the Green Man daubed on a signboard at Six Mile Bottom on the Newmarket road, the tavern suspected to be owned by the Duke of Buckingham and the Earl of Rochester, the playwright and the poet, where, desiring some lady's 'sportsman's gap', they would first intoxicate the husband. I explored the green of willow, symbol of tragic love, Burns' 'Green grow the rashes, O', the green wood of ballads and, from there, without further ado, I found myself writing my title: *The Death of Robin Hood*. Here I could further attempt to melt barriers between BC and AD, to undermine then reconstruct time.

Together with this I loved, without fully seeing, the brooding stillness of Corot and Claude, the sparkle of Canaletto, Poussin's dancers suggesting more than they reveal, the gardens, sunlit but autumnal, of Watteau, the serene splendours of Gainsborough and the observation, restrained but with powerful emotional reserves, of Richard Wilson.

Guarding my freedom like a purse, I long avoided marriage. Like, I supposed, most men I was divided, often tortuously, often hankering for the safety of immaculate promises, warm home, devoted children, sometimes repelled by all three. Much of me sympathized with Rilke's vision of partners guarding each other's loneliness, though he seemed, in practice, content to let his wife guard only her own. For myself, I needed marriage only on my own terms; having one's cake and eating it never seemed preposterous, what else was a cake for? Wodehouse's marriage seemed serenely contented but insufficiently exacting. Chekhov had written: 'I promise to be a marvellous husband, but give me a wife who is like the moon and won't appear in my sky every day.' He also warned those afraid of loneliness never to marry. Ronald Hayman's *Thomas Mann* (1966) has a most chilling sentence: 'The ambition to marry Katia Pringsheim derived partly from the books of Nietzsche and Schopenhauer that most influenced the young Thomas Mann.'

Throughout my twenties I was a sexual cruiser, like so many of my generation, having been first bedded by Tilly, an experienced, very intelligent girl with spectacular predatory instincts. Proud of this, I could not refrain from boasting, until learning that I was but one of a regiment and that her concern for hygiene was negligible.

At thirty-one I married a tall, intelligent, very loving divorcée, resembling, some said, Greta Garbo. The ceremony, in an ugly town hall, lacked pomp. 'You are now man and wife and I expect you would like to contribute towards the cost of the flowers,' the official gabbled, all in one word. I at once, though to myself alone, remembered the kernel of Kipling's generalization that, except for falling off a horse, there is nothing more fatally easy than marriage before the registrar and remarkably like going into a pawn-shop. 'But the ceremony holds and can drag a man to his undoing just as thoroughly as the "long as ye both shall live" curse from behind the altar rails.'

We were not dragged to our undoing, but I remained dogged by ambivalence, and we both, after some years, depended increasingly on off-shore support to which we eventually succumbed. We had been neither extravagantly happy nor unhappy. I eventually found happiness elsewhere; my wife, sadly, did not and died painfully.

Benedict Nicolson, whose own marriage lasted weeks rather than years, perceptively urged me to read his brother Nigel's *Portrait of a Marriage* concerning his parents, Harold Nicolson and Vita Sackville-West. At first reluctant, fearing to catch too many home truths, I at last agreed and found it moving, and indeed important, as a demonstration of what I could have achieved, the civilized happiness and intimacy possible between an intelligent and tolerant couple resolved, despite separate and unorthodox tastes, in their case sexual, to maintain and deepen more important compatibilities. 'Marriage,' they thought, 'was unnatural.'

> Marriage was only tolerable for people of strong character and independent. It was a bond which should last only as long as both wanted it to . . . But, as a happy marriage is 'the greatest of human benefits', husband and wife must strive hard for its success. Each must be subtle enough to mould their characters and behaviour to fit the other's, facet to facet, convex to concave. The husband must develop the feminine side of his nature, the wife her masculine side. He must cultivate the qualities of sympathy and intuition; she those of detachment and decision. He must respond to tears; and she must not miss trains.

Reading this, I had to admit I had followed none of it to the letter. I had given less attention to marriage than to books, gardens, social life, and my excuses were feeble. My wife once compared me to William Burroughs, though I judged this unfavourable for in 1951 he had, when drunk or high, placed a glass on his own wife's head, aimed, fired, killed her, and was forced to endure thirteen days in a Mexican gaol. But for this, he later divulged, he might never have written *The Naked Lunch*. I preferred to see myself as Shaw's 'Captain Shotover', despising happiness as a coma, manipulating loneliness.

My wife had a finer social conscience and more quickened political loyalties and antipathies than my own. She felt impelled towards marches, protests, demonstrations, while I, perhaps over-aware of the French and Russian revolutions, was sceptical of idealism, believed firmly in the supremacy of mixed motives and nodded approval for A.J.P. Taylor's quip that most historical heroes were in it for the beer. I remained attracted to the personal, singular, odd, which I observed on journeys and long solitary walks through London. In my own eyes, *The Tournament* had at last established me as a writer, author of one original book, and I surveyed the world with more assurance.

Londoners, I felt, must have changed little through the centuries:

they were still quirky, wary, disrespectful, unexpectedly confiding, as they had been in 1731, when the Abbé Prévost declared that coffee-houses and other public places were the bases of English liberty, though he was scandalized by the aristocracy sharing St James's Park with the populace and by a coffee-house where two lords, a baronet, a shoemaker, tailor, wine-merchant and other commoners exchanged the gossip of court and town.

Strangers entrusted me with uninvited, sometimes unwanted information. 'I like to be called Chief. In my special capacity, it was I who put Corsica on the map.' A builder's mate boasted that he had carved his name on Salisbury spire. I could scarcely test this but could envisage some distant cataclysm toppling the spire, unknown illiterates inspecting it and, from Carlo's hieroglyphics, deducing a lost religion. Coffee-bars and pubs, in parks, buses and ill-lit caverns catering for 'afternoon men', the absurd and dubious stacked my notebooks with the useful and occasionally the important. Ideologues talked, smote each other, debated, twisting themselves into desperate postures of conviction:

'Mozart? Dead, ain't he?'

'Josephine Baker, the black one. Left Yankee-land. When she saw the Statue of Liberty vanish, she knew she was now free.'

Characters akin to my former common-room associates abounded. Amongst writers, reviewers, hangers-on there was much to confirm a saying attributed to Confucius: there is no more enjoyable sight than that of an old friend falling off a roof. A Hyde Park tramp informed me that Ira Gershwin had been influenced by the Roman poet Horace. Painters were particularly anxious to show me their works, for which I had a formula which left them neither wholly resentful nor entirely reassured: 'Ah . . . that's the sort of painting which H.G. Wells would have studied very carefully.' Once Melnikov, an ancient Russian *émigré* sculptor, stepped out of a bar and invited Rudi Nassauer and myself 'to a dinner party in the old style'. Very stooping, very yellow, he was one of those of whom Wodehouse wrote that, looking at him, a vulture would have scented business, so would an undertaker. We were later sitting at a large table with a considerable number of writers and artists better known than ourselves in a shabby studio overcrowded with unused blocks of stone. Mel, with simian smiles, triumphantly plonked a hunk of meat on Rudi's plate: he took one bite, swore viciously and removed it to mine; briefly chewing, I hastily dumped it on the plate of my neighbour, a composer, reputedly female though her distinguishing marks were few, while she was telling C.P. Snow that he knew nothing. The meat circled the table and seemed about to begin again until Rudi flipped it unnoticed into Pamela Hansford Johnson's handbag. Melnikov, apparently unaware, offered no more food, only brandy, of such exquisiteness that we departed feeling that we had enjoyed a banquet.

I was constantly told that Marilyn Monroe was a professional role-player, assuming a multiplicity of selves. I felt this inconsiderable, something we all achieved, usually discreditably. With pupils I was glibly assertive, with publishers cringing, with editors obsequious, at literary gatherings silent, with women nervously over-talkative and, reviewing books, I liked to think industrious, tolerant, judicious, respectful to writers clearly superior to myself. In all, camouflage, self-deception, uncertainty.

Everywhere in the fifties and sixties I heard unrestrained abuse of Britain and America, lavish praise of China, Cuba, France. Cyril Connolly had written: 'The French are adults: the English, for all their natural advantages, have not grown up.' This so puzzled me that fifty years later I wrote *In Memory of England* to dispute it. Some may think me rather slow on the uptake; English stoicism had, after all, saved Connolly's bacon, while the French collapsed. For two centuries, French and Germans of impeccable culture and intellectual distinction had been discussing, analysing, resolving questions of freedom, civilization, liberty, socialism, power; but, in crisis, their institutions, and they themselves, proved irresolute. 'France' rounded up 75,000 Jews for extermination, more than the Gestapo actually demanded, and afterwards, as 'victor', demanded a place at the United Nations high table. The Irishman Beckett had a courageous record with the French Resistance attempted by few of Connolly's culture figures, save Malraux and Camus.

Much lingered from the war, still insisting on decisions. A small example occurs to me. The fascist Oswald Mosley was still campaigning for a Europe united against communism, factionalism, immigration. I was asked to a party by a rich hostess and risked bringing, uninvited, an attractive Austrian Jewess, a painter with whom I was anxious to ingratiate myself. The hostess was gracious to her. 'So good of you to come. Tom . . . do come and meet Peter and his delightful friend.'

'Tom' was Mosley, who now loomed up, striding and vigorous. He put out his hand to my delightful friend who, glaring, ignored it, then turned to me: 'Coming?'

I wavered between courtesy to my hostess, obligations to my carnality, memories of Lisa's family ending at Theresienstadt and my curiosity about Mosley himself, with whom I would have welcomed a candid exchange. Meanwhile Lisa had already gone, Mosley was gathering his coat for departure without further glance at me, and the hostess had retired to the party glittering further off. I never saw any of the three again. Dead, Master Shallow, dead.

The door had been opened by a maid: I had seen a phenomenon which, for me, was pre-war: the flash of a starched cap, the gleam of frilled cuffs, the glimmer of a prim pinafore. In my domains outright servants – chauffeurs, gardeners, maids, housekeepers, valets, skivvies – had gone. No more, even the days of Lady St Helier's childhood, when, as she put it, people had lived more simply, content with a cook, a housemaid, a parlour maid. Now, however, retainers were sidling back with different titles though with similar duties, less one-sidedly negotiated. They had become staff, home help, the au-pair, domestic superintendent, private assistant, home consultant, even, in one household I knew of, attaché. Au pairs, often from Scandinavia, were numerous, coldly beautiful, acquisitive, liable to early pregnancy, apt to disappear, a few perishing atrociously. The attaché was hired by a publisher with the soubriquet of Mr Strictly Speaking: 'Strictly speaking, her work's no good', 'Strictly speaking, the Nazis were the first to refine killing into an art'; his tone suggesting that minor alternatives existed, but conscience demanded he reject them.

At this time, during the Cold War, my pupils and friends professed sleepless anxieties about the Bomb. I did not. I had been the same during the Blitz, when on fire duties I clung to an unfinished novel or the one gathering dust in some publisher's cupboard and was anxious to survive if not the war at least until the next week which could provide the marvellous acceptance or the end of a promising chapter. Now, a dozen years on, I must finish, Bomb or no Bomb, my novel, my review, my small travel piece which so few would read. I must admit that I had rejoiced at Hiroshima. Many friends from school and Oxford were fighting in Asia, and mass destruction of the enemy would surely save them from torture and death. I doubt whether many then disagreed with me. Later, in the *Observer*, 6 September 1959, Clem Attlee wrote that in 1945 Truman, Churchill and himself were ignorant of the genetic effects of atomic disaster. When a youngish novelist wrote in the press that he agonized night and day about the Bomb, I thought, unfairly, of some lines in an Ezra Pound canto:

> Yuan Yan sat by the roadside pretending to receive wisdom
> And Kung said
> 'You old fool, come out of it,
> Get up and do something useful.'

My wife and I were moved by Doris Lessing's play, *Each His Own Wilderness*, which reproduces the fifties atmosphere. In it, beneath the liberal chatter, a youth dreams of the cold, white cackle of electricity as the Bomb explodes, the curved globe burns, half of it already torn apart. My wife shuddered and wept that night, but from introspection, solipsism or lack of compassion I gave the almighty Bomb scarcely a thought, despite her pleadings that I should use my imagination. I did not believe in a likely catastrophe, save for one instant during the 1962 Cuban missile crisis. This was not due to any trust in human reason or rulers' regard for self-preservation; the whim of a benighted fundamentalist, the accident of a misunderstood code, some grotesque absurdity might indeed spark off disaster, Ragnarok, but, more probable, was ambush on a darkened street, a fainting fit on a station platform, even snake-bite on a Dorset heath or plausible arrest for an imaginary crime. Meanwhile . . .

I was more disturbed by Vladimir's lament in *Waiting for Godot*: 'The air is full of our cries.' Unforgettable – though this adjective at once recalls W.B. Yeats beginning a lecture with, 'First, I must quote you that unforgettable sonnet by Rossetti . . . er . . . which for the moment I've forgotten.'

Ultimately, the Bomb became a private joke between my wife and myself. We had a friend, a gifted pianist, billed for his first concert but afflicted with nervousness. The evening came, the hall was filled, he was terrified but calmed himself with a remedy not yet, perhaps, repeated. The audience waited. Finally, the manager stalked forward to announce that a bomb had been planted. Would we all wait outside. After ten minutes he reappeared. The bomb had been discovered and removed and, despite damage to his nerves, the artiste would at once perform. Mountainous applause, redoubled when he trotted in. Henceforward if he hit only one correct note in fifteen he could do no wrong; he scored most notes correctly, the evening was triumphant.

7

MOVEMENTS

Don't trust too much in books: they only share
what has been and will be. Try to be stronger,
grasp something that now is. And then no longer
your ripeness will be all.

– Rilke

IN my later thirties, I still felt myself young, eager to grasp the
idiosyncracies, absurdities, small ravages visible on all sides. A
fashion was prevailing in restricted circles for Mao's *Little Red Book*,
stuffed with platitudes, unaccompanied by references to famine, heresy
hunts, executions, sexual bullying, failure, the customary graveyard fancies of the one-party state and its leaders. The Marxist Eric Hobsbawm –
a charming man, who shares my pleasure in Offenbach – conceded in
1997 that Mao's Cultural Revolution was barbarous and lunatic. The
Chairman's 'chauvinistic arrogance' made Khrushchev shiver, as his
own recommendation for peaceful coexistence was rejected, and he
was urged to provoke the West into war. Some 700,000 of the Chinese
intelligentsia were reported to have been exterminated between 1957 and
1969, while millions perished of hunger during the unnecessary and
futile Great Leap Forward.

I have always found China, like Russia, arouses strong, sometimes contradictory feelings. In his memoirs of 1953 Hugh Dalton mentioned that Beatrice Webb disliked the Chinese for their devastating common sense; simultaneously, she admired them for reverence to ancestors, 'the Emperor' and for scientific method.

I had to guard myself against cynicism and negation. Ideology and patent-medicine policies were not for me, and, after a momentary season of wholesale indignation, I no longer felt seamed by guilt for the misfortunes of Nottingham garment workers in 1826 or by the enormities of the Empire. I preferred a solid front door to organized love and dogmatic ukases from those who mistook slogans and bureaucratic incompetence for serious government. Yet I jibbed at remaining aloof, like a batsman in his prime not disdaining to slog but finding excuses to avoid playing. In the callow conceit of youth, I once convinced myself that a high-spirited article of my own, in *Tribune* in 1945, had been responsible for the establishment of Israel. I was thus tempted to list myself as 'statesman' on my passport, its final substitute, 'writer' being frequently mistaken for 'waiter'. I joined some committees, attended a few conferences, feeling markedly out of place, attempted to co-ordinate active politics with history and journalistic exposures, in *A Sort of Forgetting*, strove to keep myself at concert pitch for the fight against the false and unfair.

Suez, Budapest, Prague still remain in the public memory; much else is forgotten. There was the Stalinist Hungarian police chief, Gabor Peter, who loved gardening, 'especially pruning'. He had arrested the Primate Cardinal Mindszenty and successfully conspired against his rival, Lazlo Rajk, promising a light sentence and safety for his family in return for a false confession of having collaborated with Tito, Britain and America (his signature swiftly followed by his execution). This and Russian bad faith in Hungary in 1956 inspired my novel *A Safe Conduct*, set in fifteenth-century Germany. Gabor Peter, in his turn, was overtaken by other rivals, accused of torture, beatings, 5,000 deaths, of spying for Britain and Israel; he was gaoled, eventually released, ending as a librarian.

Periodically I met Robert Conquest, soft-spoken poet and chronicler of Stalinist oppression, now reporting the strikes occurring in the post-Stalin Russian empire, suppressed by mass executions.

Incredible times. In McCarthyite America, in Soviet Europe, writers who put themselves at risk by publishing included Arthur Miller, as well as Sinyavsky, Djilas, Daniel, Solzhenitsyn. In Britain we risked nothing, though a number of writers assured us otherwise. Aneurin Bevan had called the British press the most prostituted in the world, as though he were oblivious to the journalists proscribed, imprisoned, shot, denied publication in numerous one-party states, whose newspapers were merely standardized communiqués. Future Foreign Secretary, he disqualified himself by such ignorance of foreign conditions. As late as 1986 Harold Pinter, discussing his play *Mountain Language*, declared: 'The play is about the suppression of language and the loss of freedom of expression . . . a number of Kurds have said that the play touches them and their lives. But I believe it also reflects what's happening in England today – the suppression of ideas, speech, thought.'

In reality, the censorship that I found myself actually encountering came from Pinter's own camp, with my socialist-controlled local council banning *The Times*, the *Spectator*, the *Daily Telegraph* and selected books from its libraries until successfully taken to court.

I always voted for the individual, not the party, according to circumstances. In my youth George Lansbury, selfless and humane Labour leader, wanted to abolish the air force while Hitler was coming to power, promising war. Lansbury might earlier have secured my vote, though not in 1940. I disliked labels – 'worker', 'bourgeois', 'the class struggle'. Visibly, the majority seemed content to try to join those slightly better-off than themselves, and I agreed with my London School of Economics friend Professor Kenneth Minogue, who wrote in *Encounter*: 'The proletariat is, of course, a particularly vulnerable ideological concept and may easily be recognized as a concept composed by intellectuals anxious to play a role in politics.'

As early as 1937 I distrusted the teachings of Douglas Jay's *The Socialist Case* that in nutrition, health, education 'the gentleman from Whitehall really does know better what is good for people than the people know themselves'. I felt more at ease with A.J.P. Taylor, who held that the basis of modern democracy is that men do not believe what they say. I wondered about Aneurin Bevan who, during the Suez Crisis, publicly denounced Anthony Eden and privately called Nasser an Egyptian sewer-rat; who, when out of office, denounced Britain's atomic bomb and, in office, retained it. There were always private incongruities behind official announcements. An ambassador in Moscow was recalled in 1968 after, as we all assumed, protesting against the Russian invasion of Prague – actually, after admitting an affair with a Russian servant. I was intrigued by the Romanian ex-President Ceaucescu's protest when, with himself, his wife was condemned to death: 'But she's a graduate!' I was astonished that the famous cricketers Alec and Eric Bedser, at thirty-one, were unable to afford a bathroom.

Much remained hidden in the esoteric realms of military, nuclear and cartel complexes. In 1997 I read in Eric Hobsbawm's *On History*: 'We now know, thanks to the disclosures of President Clinton's administration, the USA engaged, from shortly after the war until well into the 1970s, in systematic radiation experiments on human beings, chosen from amongst those felt to be of socially inferior value.' From 1935 until 1976 Social Democratic Sweden was not alone in sterilizing and incarcerating 'vagrants', the physically handicapped and undesirable radical types; the Swiss practised similar policies, also the Norwegians, beginning with gypsies and sexual deviants. Socialists excused all this as protection of working-class health.

In the 1960s the existence of such individuals as Raoul Wallenberg was not fully realized. This young Swedish diplomat, today commemorated by a London statue, had rescued 70,000 of the 100,000 Hungarian Jews still surviving in Nazi-controlled Hungary by coolly handing out Swedish passports. He was helped by the Papal Nuncio and by Roosevelt's threat in June 1944 to bomb Budapest unless the death-train to Auschwitz ceased. The war ending, Wallenberg was summoned to meet the Russian authorities and has never been seen again.

It was all part of that shadowy history, outside school books, of international power blocs, regional baronies, multi-purpose corporations and arms cartels, often larger, richer, better armed than national states. To greed for money, power, flesh must be added the more subtle seductions of Hermes, enjoyment of mischief, delight in others' discomfiture, practical joking, more for its own sake than for riches. Too hastily, with inadequate knowledge and method, insufficiently detached, I attempted to focus this in *A Sort of Forgetting*.

This novel, though ambitious and well-intentioned, was my worst failure, though, like *Enemies*, it rewarded me with a gratifying postscript. In it I had praised Bishop Graf Clemens August von Galen, Bishop of Münster, where once the Anabaptists had raged, slung texts towards heaven and slaughtered in God's name. The bishop denounced the Nazis from the pulpit, even in wartime distributed subversive sermons throughout northern Germany, with such grand panache that the SS dared not arrest him. I had also mentioned the White Rose, a group of Munich students who bravely handed out anti-Nazi leaflets denouncing the wanton sacrifice of 330,000 at Stalingrad, the extermination of the Polish aristocracy and of Jews: 'Why are the Germans so apathetic when confronted by such dreadful and disgraceful crimes?' They exploded a bomb during a *Gauleiter*'s speech. Amongst the leaders were Hans Scholl and his sister Sophie, soon shot for treason. Sophie, though absent from the bomb-setting, demanded to be treated like the others: 'I hope that my name will always be associated with the first attempt of German students to liberate themselves.' She and her friends remained obdurate in resolution and hope. 'What does our own death matter, if thousands are stirred up, awoken by our action? The students are bound to rebel.'

The students did not rebel, and a few days after the executions they assembled to applaud the man who had betrayed the conspirators.

An extract from *A Sort of Forgetting* ultimately reached a surviving sister, Inge Richer-Scholl, who had herself been a political prisoner. In memory of the White Rose she founded in 1950 the Geschwister-Scholl-Stiftung to foster regeneration of freedom, social and cultural responsibilities, ever-watchful for bigots, dogmatists, despots. There had been such a school in my novel; international, humanist, tolerant.

I felt rather spuriously ennobled on receiving a letter from Inge, in which she told me that von Galen's sermons 'were famous for the help which poured out of them for a lot of helpless and undecided people'. My wretched novel had not been wholly in vain. 'It makes me feel that the spirit of goodwill and real and practical renovation is working and alive above all what happens in the present; that nothing has been useless, even if for a time it seems so.'

That paragon, the Great Man, so extolled by Rudi Nassauer, had righteously disapproved of my book and lectured me rather severely on the arts of writing. As if summoning unnecessary reinforcements for an army already victorious, he then surprised me by granting me his opinion of the stories of W. Somerset Maugham. 'They are not pleasing, they are not pertinent to one's real interests, they are not true; they are simply graphic and plausible, like a bit of a dream that one might drop into in an afternoon nap. Why read it? I suppose it is to make money, because writing stories is a profession.'

I subsequently discovered that the Great Man had not improvised this but quoted, word perfect, from George Santayana. Meanwhile, to avoid a quarrel, I told him Maugham's account of Edmund Gosse praising his first novel, *Liza of Lambeth*, in 1897. He would meet Gosse once or twice a year for twenty years, and Gosse always said to him: 'Ah, my dear Maugham, I liked your Liza of Lambeth so much. How wise of you never to have written anything else.'

Maugham, by most accounts, was not a good man, not even very likeable, and appeared, from a safe distance, cold, supercilious, selfish. He wrote a paragraph which, during the era of Kitchen Sink, Angry Young Men, Theatre of Cruelty, I would hear, demonstrated hypocritical mawkishness, an outrage on the transcendent seriousness of literature and art:

Art, unless it leads to right action, is no more than the opium of an intelligentsia. It is not in art that one may hope to find some assuagement to the pessimism that long ago found expression in the Book of Ecclesiastes. I think there is in the heroic courage with which man confronts the irrationality of the world a beauty greater than the beauty of art. I find it in the defiant gesture of Paddy Finucane when, plunging to his death, he transmitted a message to his squadron: 'This is it, chaps.' I find it in the cool determination of Captain Oates when he went out to his death in the Antarctic night rather than be a burden to his comrades. I find it in the loyalty of Helen Vagliano, a woman not very young, not very pretty, not very intelligent, who suffered hellish torture and accepted death for a country not her own, rather than betray her friends.

Having abandoned teaching in 1963, I had to seek survival in petty journalism and lecturing. Sometimes fees, minuscule though they were, had to be extracted by cunning, entailing some ill will. Once, at the Ethical Hall, after I finished speaking on what I imagined as ethics, the promoter inquired whether I really wished to accept the agreed fee or, more likely, would prefer a slender book on political morality written by himself. Adroitly I countered by telling him that, like all right-thinking people, I had of course already purchased his admirable publication. This he heard without gratification, though, after some delay, he coughed up a cheque. Whenever possible I went north, indulging my love of lonely tarns, tiny fishing ports, island ferries, half-imaginary forests, generous hospitality from free spirits.

Two such forays are typical. In one I had lectured on Arthurian myth to a small audience near Kelso, and, offered hospitality by an unknown woman, was sitting tired, even discouraged, in a long, expensive car, a chauffeur driving me through hills, now grey and steep, now green and smooth, before reaching a castellated pile graciously stationed amongst lawns and trees, a rough border keep to which had been added spacious eighteenth-century embellishments.

The elderly chatelaine was brisk with no-nonsense welcome, but then added, 'I do hope you won't mind, but I have invited our Presbyterian minister to join us for dinner.'

I had spontaneously liked Mrs Mac, but at this my feelings again slumped. I did mind, very much; friendly talk over choice food would be imperilled by some decrepit bigot, spiritual descendent of ferocious Knox, stuffed with fury against colour and sin. I awaited the evening ahead like a sulky child planning world destruction with a box of matches, ready to summon a yellow playfellow whose breath is terrible.

My case had been unpacked, spring flowers arranged at varying levels, a window opened, through which I could see beyond the park to moors, purplish slopes bleached with new lambs. Throughout my stay I was to have sensations of unseen service, clothes brushed, flowers changed, meals appearing as if out of the air. As in my childhood at Bletsoe, flimsy presences, soundless, gliding, were half glimpsed in passages, already vanished, gathering true substance only by my stepping outside the enchanted walls. Upstairs would be the long-remembered attics piled with Edwardian gowns and straw hats, Victorian doll's houses, hobby-horses, battledores; downstairs would be panelled halls and long galleries loaded with doubtful ancestral master-pieces, tall porcelain vases and polished ornamented chairs, the heavy chest in which a child had crouched for hide-and-seek, discovered, of course, but two centuries later, the chapel, dedicated perhaps to St Uncumber who, to protect her virginity, sprouted a beard. Dreading going down to dinner to meet the Calvinist persecutor, witch-hunter, destroyer of art and decency, I remembered Mrs Feargus, a boiled-looking gardener's wife, describing my mother's friend's pregnancy as a purse filled by a refined personage.

I at last went below, hoping for strong drink. Mrs Mac had a repu-tation for hospitality, but I now imagined her as some crone crouching at a crossroads with an evil, impossible riddle. In green gown, long black skirt, grey piled hair alight with tiny diamonds, she now, in reality, looked younger, her blue eyes, still bright and full, greeting me from above a barely visible network of lines with cheery camaraderie.

'Ah, Peter, come along in. I hope you're not one for herbal tea and dry biscuits, and that you're as greedy for the malt as Adam and I always are.'

Relieved, I saw that the foul minister had not yet arrived. Adam, possibly her son, was a burly, rough-edged, yellow-jerseyed youth who had been at my lecture. He shook hands, then concluded some dis-cussion with Mrs Mac about Graham Greene: 'I particularly like his description of the African girl, smiling like an open piano.'

He grinned at me, his pink face shy, as if it were fumbling. 'Of course . . . you yourself . . .' Confused, he hastily handed me another drink so that I was sitting with a full glass in either hand, and we were immedi-ately laughing with an immoderation that would have scandalized the latecomer.

Outside, between blue and silver curtains, daffodils misted as the sun drooped over the hills. Mrs Mac spoke of the local council, which she headed. 'If you're going to partake at all, go for the top. With a sharp knife for the red tape. We've had a problem which might interest you, Peter. The headship of our village school. Only two candidates. One, a wretched teacher but a Conservative lay reader, very pious. The other a Marxist atheist, marvellous with children. I don't need to tell you whom Adam and I chose. Mind . . .' The blue eyes were slightly teasing, as though I had expostulated on behalf of wretched teaching and piety. 'We are apt to get our own way. It needs a bit of management, but these things always do. I don't like dictatorship, I do enjoy management. You would probably call it manipulation. Well, that's a thought. The others were a mite resentful, Adam being in holy orders and it's a manse school. But they all rather enjoy coming here for dinner – Charlotte's cooking, which we hope you're going to approve of. We do confess to a bit of feudalism in these wee acres.'

These acres, I discovered, were seven thousand, which Mrs Mac had supervised since her husband's death in the First World War. She had recently learnt to fly, the better to supervise. I observed later that the maids and landworkers all called her Elizabeth but were expected to do a very full day's work. Meanwhile Adam grinned at me, as if at practices unseemly, reprehensible but not in these parts criminal. His words were at odds with his bucolic, slightly unfinished features and undergraduate casualness. 'All men are my brothers, they are not always my friends. I know you've been a teacher, so don't be offended when I mention Sri Aurobindo once saying that the first principle of education is that nothing can be taught.'

I was immensely relieved, after initial surprise, that Adam's holy orders were compatible with learning, sympathy and humour. He had read Rilke and we joined in chanting the opening of 'Childhood':

> School, School! The anguish and the weariness!
> The waiting and the downright stupid things!
> O Loneliness, O Time with broken wings . . .

At dinner, served as though by hands without bodies, excellent wines accompanied salmon, game, summer pudding awash with cream, soused with Cointreau, presented, I suspected, by dutiful peasantry – and indeed Mrs Mac disclosed that, formally, she had every year to oblige the Queen of Scotland with a rose, a kiss and a roebuck.

Adam, referring to my lecture, already in far-off haze, discussed the connection, revived by T.S. Eliot, of Christ with a tiger, an appropriate symbol, he thought, sometimes replaced by that of a panther, the Saviour and the animal alike suggesting agility, some deviousness and considerable menace. He told me a legend of Christ blinding a beggar for carelessly obstructing him at a well. Prompted by Mrs Mac he described inspecting an oriental tomb advertised as that of a saint, prayers to whom would relieve drought, colic and malice from barren ladies. A Syrian, resplendent in white shorts and dinner-jacket displaying the ribbon of the Légion d'Honneur, had shaken his head then, very smoothly, saying: 'Stupid superstition, of course. You and I are men of the world. The tomb is said to cover a thermal spring fixed as a cure-all by extortionate priests and their catamites and identified as Alph, your man Coleridge's sacred river. The larger truth is more interesting. There is no water there at all but a path leading direct to hell, and for a small fee, tax deductable as charity, I can supply the evidence.'

The trees rustled, a bird flew. Following a query from Mrs Mac I repeated the legend of King Arthur drowning May-born children after an oracle foretold his own killing by a May child. Adam leant forward with a scholar's intensity: 'That's interesting. I seem to remember Mordred being born in May.'

Over brandy, by candlelight, silver spots glinting around us on different levels, satisfied, intimate, we leisurely exchanged fragments of the bizarre but not always nonsensical. An Edinburgh impresario had recently claimed membership of a secret society founded by Marlowe in 1583. Mrs Mac sighed, before mentioning Susan, 'down the road' – some seventy miles away – and her shadowy companion, Miss Beatrice, born in 1730. Miss Elode, on the estate, spent long hours in a locked room with her father, killed at Ypres. At Glenluce a monkey forged an abbot's signature. Following the birth of ninety-nine daughters from numerous obedient girls the McNab had a son. I spoke of my much-loved school friend, Ian Souter, drowned in India in 1942, and my recurrent dream of him asking me to telephone him. I lose his number but, after a frantic search, find one, possibly his, then awake. I then ring it, usually it is non-existent, but twice voices have answered, both different but belonging to someone named Ian.

Next morning I found the breakfast-room: silver and pewter dishes and salvers on a black sideboard, a Hanoverian coffee-pot gleaming above a loaf shaped like a beehive, thick wads of butter, many jams in porcelain jars. I was alone, though a place had been laid for Mrs Mac. Tempted by aromas, I uncovered the various dishes: sausages, bacon, bubble-and-squeak, eggs scrambled, poached, boiled. I ate, and, as Mrs Mac still did not come, I ate again, then realized in shuddering dismay that I had scoffed the lot.

Toast and coffee dried on me. Feeling watched by the hidden and sardonic, I awaited the footsteps on stairs, then, in slow motion, the door opening, Mrs Mac primed with morning greeting, then, in monstrous, fatal quiet, lifting one cover after another, seeking some scrap of food.

Mrs Mac ignored the sideboard. 'I'm so glad you feel at home here and haven't waited about for me. Alas, I only have a little coffee at this hour. Now, it's a lovely morning, I do hope you will allow me to drive you around, to show off our patch of Scotland.'

Eschewing the plane, selecting a car, she did so. The day opened to hills, skies, fleeing hares, Mrs Mac allowing me my own dreaminess. Hares: moon hares, changing sex twice yearly, feared by pregnant girls; Jack hares squatting in circles, avoided by fisher-folk and with a human-like shriek when hunted; Anne Boleyn, witch queen, transformed to a hare. A hill cave ahead could be the mouth of Uffern, Celtic underworld. I was happy with the new light, the softness of April leaf. 'Then lay my head in Avalon that day.' The air was wrinkled with birdsong in a morning of quiet talk on sun-strewn uplands, short cool valleys, a ring of scarred boulders, perhaps runic, each leaning slightly inwards as if fearing to be overheard. Adam had quoted a Scottish poet, 'Everything is sweetened by risk', but for this day I risked nothing. I was not to be blinded by a terrorist howling for rights he cannot describe, or describes too easily, or overthrown by a neglected paving-stone. All that awaited me down south was my novel *The Wall*, published in 1990, evocation of a creeping Roman pessimism in which defence can be imprisonment, government paralysis, a mighty city strangled by its own bureaucratic guts.

On another Scottish journey I accompanied Peregrine Worsthorne for his journalistic fact-finding, a happy week of contrasts, of ship-building yards and a lonely stone-circle, the Edinburgh Mile and the austere St Magnus' Cathedral on Orkney, Clydeside agitators, a duke in his dukery, rough Glasgow pubs and superb fat kippers at Fitzroy Maclean's hotel on Loch Fyne, all with Perry's probing, teasing, inspiriting talk and small, memorable occasions. For one, we were booked to visit two ladies of distinguished lineage. On the way we passed an ancient tower where there had once lived a friend of my mother's. Doctor, musicologist, literary scholar, local historian, he had further repute: whenever I mentioned his name – at a PEN conference in New York, in a Madrid bar, at Warsaw, Florence and Bournemouth – someone always said, 'Wasn't that the man who murdered his wife?', the tone more that of a statement than question. Remembering his talk, subtle, irritable, with many examples of human misbehaviour exhibited in unusual, sometimes exotic ways, I did not doubt it.

Meanwhile, Perry was giving me instructions with unaccustomed severity. 'Now you're not to eat too much at tea. It will spoil your appetite for the rather good dinner we're likely to get at the Lothians.'

We arrived, we passed between suits of armour, to meet the ladies. One was pretty, one was plain, almost galleon-shaped. Claiming his due, Perry appropriated the former, at once indulging his zest for serious talk – the influence of the grand piano on the advance of Islam or some such topic – while my companion turned to me. 'Please help.'

There appeared no imminent danger, but of course I nodded. Her face, ovalled, slightly askew, grimaced wildly. 'Tell me. Does Mr Worsthorne like cake?'

'Of course he does. He eats very little else.' The face straightened. 'I am so glad. So very glad. You see, I spent all yesterday . . .'

Glistening, white as Antarctica, reddened with cherries, greened with strips of angelica, tinged with apricot, mellow with sultanas, the cake was indeed a masterpiece, a short cut to the ends of the earth. Perry, however, his speech gaining pace, submitting significant details, only glanced at it as he might an impertinent heckler, then waved it away, 'No, no . . . now can you really believe . . .'

From courtesy, from loyalty, I had to eat almost the entire cake: it was rich, moist, could have graced any Victorian murder by poison or Captain Hook's table, but at dinner I had to forgo course after course, each of ascending magnificence.

Throughout my life I found excuses to wander: to Tooting Bec, to Cornwall, to Ledbury, to Banbury, to Lancaster, down frowsty alleys and along wet, glistening pavements, through depths of greens and whites, between hedges, awaiting whatever they offered: the trivial, the ludicrous, the distinctive. I once passed a village house apparently inhabited by Mrs Smith. Mrs Smith? Ah, but she had once been nationally famous, as Ethel le Neve, supporting star of one of the most sensational murders of the century. Disguised, very inadequately, as a boy, she had fled with her lover, Dr H.H. Crippen, 'Mr Robinson and son', on SS *Montrose*. On the voyage, admiring the ship's new radio, Crippen observed to the captain, 'How privileged we are to be alive in an age of such scientific marvels!' His enthusiasm was misplaced. Captain Kendall had noticed some surreptitious fondlings, a heavy bulge in Mr Robinson's pocket. Warned by radio, the American police were waiting, and Crippen was hanged at Pentonville for wife murder, having penned farewell verses to Ethel:

> When the heart is breaking, and the way is long,
> In seeking rest, with no accompanying song,
> Scorned by the world, by cruel fate undone,
> Friendless, yet not alone – for there is one –
> Who truly loves this soon committed clay,
> Who truly dreads this sure and awful day
> When mortal soul shall fly to realms aloft,
> In life-and-death she still shall speak me soft.

Unable to glimpse the recluse, I bought locally, at first-hand cost, a second-hand copy of Ernest Raymond's novel, *We the Accused*, centred on Crippen, le Neve and Bella Crippen, once a minor music-hall singer.

Like F. Tennyson Jesse's *A Pin to See the Peep-Show*, re-enacting the Thompson–Bywaters murder, the book powerfully affected me and still does.

The more I journeyed, the more distrustful I became of generalizations, the more significant appeared exceptions. The Gentleman, the Exploiter, the Leader were types, not classes. In a Cumbrian fishing village I found women almost all-powerful; in a Welsh mining valley less so. About a mining dispute, interpreted by many newspapers as capital versus labour, symptoms of class war, I found much to confirm the opinion of Fernando Henriques:

> It transpired that part of the resentment directed against Italian miners was engendered by their very different attitude to women. They treated them as individuals to be courted and wooed. While it would be too extreme to suggest that the attitude of the Yorkshire miner towards sex is necessarily brutal, there is little scope in his *Weltanschauung* for sexual finesse.

At Aldershot I sat in a cheap cinema where soldiers spat with laughter at *Brief Encounter*; amongst teenagers at Colchester jeering at *The Diary of Anne Frank*; with hundreds of pupils weeping in sympathy for the doomed Führer, as portrayed by Alec Guinness in *The Last Days of Hitler*. Near Diss an old man, barred from pubs for his vicious temper, stared at a great oak on a hillside. Was it true that he could neither read nor write? He gestured morosely at the oak: 'I can read this, can't I?'

A pub often gave a coda to a day of solitude and reverie. Once I listened to a large, mottled man lecturing a friend, who allowed him the fitful attention of a prompter during a long run.

'I'm an Essex man, as we both know. Thorpe-le-Soken. You won't know it, but Jack the Ripper's buried there. I'd better not tell you his name, for several very good reasons, but he was one of the royal physicians, the Queen's, Victoria of course, not the present lass. He was also a goodish painter and philanthropist, alms-giver, do-gooder, call it what you like. High-minded into the bargain. Acting on a royal hint, for Victoria deplored girls of a certain nature, the said doctor cruised

Whitechapel in a closed carriage, killing them with considerable grace, perhaps charm. When all's said and done, I suppose, it wasn't quite the thing.'

There was always an imaginary landscape, sometimes desolate, spiked by an occasional castle or smudged forest, soundless, as if transfixed by a spell; sometimes green and watery, with gardens, fountains, clipped hedges. I might see it in movies by Cocteau, Carné, Bergman; in a Rilke poem, 'In spite of all, we are the heirs of those gardens of infinite singing.' I sought small, provincial foreign towns, drowsy for years, then swept by riot, unforseen, unexplained, dispersing as swiftly as it began. I brooded over people crowding a bleak, nameless station because, after so many years of nothingness, a train was rumoured to be approaching. I had my French and German landscapes; my Russian, in which seasons pushed themselves to extremes, sportsmen lay in dawn marshes for the flying duck and remembered their youth, riding in the Caucasus; amongst the raspberries a languorousorous Anna Petrovna murmurs 'Will he come?' to her parasol, and a tutor – myself – flourishes amongst bored married ladies. And those heady spring thaws, that birch solitary under a putty sky or throwing out silver under deep and thrilling blue.

Under stress, through failed loves and rejections, an ill-conceived book, physical pain, I was humiliated to realize how little great art and literature could comfort me. More healing was kindness from an imagined enemy, a chance invitation, even a sunlit morning.

Best of all was travel, usually undertaken on impulse. There were always small adventures, incidents tiny yet lodging within me. In Stockholm a limousine briefly halted outside our house; a small girl clamoured excitedly, 'Orson Welles!' She rushed down, slunk back, face like a frost-bitten dahlia. 'Orson Welles?' 'No, it's only the King!' On a Swedish island, recovering from a breakdown less tragic than I had thought, I would wander the woods for wild strawberries, 'old men of the woods', then lie down naked to sleep in the long grass beneath leaves. One day some villagers visited me. 'We are delighted, sir, to have you amongst us. You write, you read, you prosper. For these, we admire you. We also admire your courage.'

Courage? Surely not.

'You must know, sir, that for two hundred years our children have been forbidden these woods. The snakes . . .'

My reputation for courage vanished; but my wandering instinct remained. I was never the cultured sightseer; to walk in Lapland under the midnight sun suited me better than to read Strindberg's tormented masterpieces or gaze at his stormy paintings. With no knowledge of foreign languages I responded more intently to shape, design, gesture, atmosphere. I never visited the Louvre or Notre Dame but, trailed by Jean Sablon's song 'La Chanson des Rues', happily lost myself in parks and side streets, suddenly chancing upon the statue of Danton, of Balzac, the unexpectedness renewing my vitality, sensations of marvellous freedom enveloping me as I strolled through jabbering crowds, understanding none of the jabber. I accumulated a store of details, gifts from Hermes, so that I still see the Roman aqueduct towering over Segovia, an unearthly ride through moonlit nights; a golden wall at Smolensk, before which even Napoleon removed his hat without asking himself what he was doing there; the massed columns and double arches within the mosque-cathedral, Cordoba, lights and shadows in endless dance; old men reading in the great mosque at Damascus; a tomb of John the Baptist loaded with gifts from the faithful – a tiara, a packet of Enos, a suitcase, a tin of sweets; another sacred tomb, draped with a poster for *It Started with Eve* starring Charles Laughton and Deanna Durbin. Tolstoy's Moscow house, his wife's drawing-room, 'the Dull Room', reserved for bores, and a bicycle sent him by Birmingham workers; a tourist staring at Mont Blanc and exclaiming that it reminded her of Devonshire; a fox near Poznan shining in sunlight fleeing between golden blocks of grain, dense as if in a Brueghel painting. I would sit in the Pitti garden above Florence, with red wine, writing *The Story Teller*, the hills and dome glittering now soft, now fierce, towards sunset.

In Paris I sat with elderly Russians in a faded salon crammed with miniatures, sepia photographs, yellowed books, antique relics of tsarist lives. Understanding little, I again felt myself in history, nourished by nostalgia, discontent and the fragrance of past occasions and forgotten grandees. Several, stately as camels, never spoke, but they were not dull;

they made me understand the force of 'eloquent silence', 'ugly silence', even 'hangman's silence'. I now understand better the rabbi in Elie Weisel's *All Rivers Run to the Sea*, who remained silent even when speaking. At Saint Cloud I was received in a decrepit château by an old lady who had known George Moore and Nancy Cunard. She told me of a previous owner, a rich and beautiful woman known as the Cat with the Crimson Claws. She married a handsome illiterate who hated books, fearing they possessed black magic. At his dictation she wrote her will in his favour. A year later, in 1957, she was found strangled in a ditch. Her husband was acquitted and, having brandished the will, celebrated with a party that lasted four days but was then confronted by a second and later will, more grammatically phrased, in which the fortune was left not to him but to his birthplace, with instructions to the mayor to establish a public library in her husband's name. Maugham out of Maupassant, my hostess said, admiring neither.

I was happy in Austria, with the Wednesday evening organ recitals at St Stephen's, Vienna, packed with young people perched on altars, fonts, steps, rapt as Bach thundered around us. I walked above Salzburg on a mountain named 'the Sorrows of the Retired Ladies'; I found memories of Franz Josef at Bad Ischl and, as if ambushed, stumbled against a bronze statue of him in local costume standing over a dead stag in the forest. In one palace, a clock, fashioned like a golden bird, at each hour dropped the appropriate number of pearls into a jewelled bowl.

In Geneva I was staying with a rich friend. Over evening drinks we were disturbed by one of his staff. 'I beg your pardon, sir, but I think both you gentlemen might be interested to know that Kennedy, er, Mr Kennedy, that is to say, the President of the United States, has been shot . . . he is, so to speak, dead.'

Julio at once rushed to the telephone, not, as, in my innocence, I supposed, anxious to console the widow but in anxiety about the state of the market.

Staying in Warsaw I just saved myself from a dreadful gaffe. A museum curator showed me some paintings; they were garish, rudimentary in design, violent in comment. I suddenly realized their origin. They were a last witness to the sufferings in the Warsaw Ghetto.

The customary mingling of normality and fantasy was seldom absent. One autumn I was in a car accompanying a young writer to Berne, where his wife was eagerly, even desperately awaiting him – they had been married only the previous week. Halting at Brussels, we could not resist a Bosch–Brueghel exhibition. Entering side by side, we were at once wildly applauded for, together, we were the millionth visitor. This delayed us three days; we were hauled to radio, to television, to banquets, lunch with the Regent, to local salons, seminars, editorial offices. Charles was too nervous to contact his now frantic bride, leaving me to ring her almost hourly, my excuses sounding ever more improbable, almost surreal, impairing her regard for me to this day.

Near Gmunden I stayed with a French family, living in some manner of exile. The father had been a judge, still relishing the executions he had fixed, particularly in Algeria. He had a downcast wife and two sons, all muscle and brawn, whom he hated, not allowing them to marry. Yet he was exceptionally tender with his daughter, who had Down's syndrome. He would sit, glad, even proud of her as she paddled in dirty water and destroyed her mother's flowers. Early in my sojourn he assaulted his wife for what was, admittedly, a most unsavoury lunch. We then discovered that the daughter had thrown detergent into the casserole, at which the judge chuckled immoderately then went almost tearful in loving appreciation.

In America, on Greyhound buses moving south through scores of inert townships, youths lounging at gas stations and drug-stores, through lonely farmlands, I felt myself the enigmatic stranger in a B-movie arriving to face, or cause, trouble. I had also found that to sit alone in Washington Square guaranteed constant visitations from the indigent, the ferocious, the young. One wanted to read me 'a longish poem I've tried out' – most of the *Iliad*; another demanded that I finance a film script of international significance; a third, black, perhaps teenaged, announced without embarrassment that he was Mr Saul Bellow, so that I might possibly . . .

Once, in 1960 in Paris, at behest of Emanuel Litvinoff, I 'represented Britain', along with himself, Wolf Mankowitz and Muriel Spark, at an international conference on the anti-Semitism rife in the Soviet state.

The Stalinist writer Ilya Ehrenburg appeared in my hotel room around midnight, attempting to convince me of the righteousness of his masters. There was no Russian religious intolerance, there was no political intolerance, there was no anti-Semitism, only Western propaganda. All Jews were happy; there were no Jews. The Soviet constitution was the most advanced democratic document yet known, the most positive guarantee of freedom of conscience, beliefs, individual rights. I could only tell him to listen to the conference and hear of ravaged synagogues and theatres, proscribed newspapers and closed schools, children, intellectuals, families persecuted.

The conference itself was supported by Schweitzer, Mauriac, Russell, Eleanor Roosevelt. Of the many speeches I remember only Lionel Trilling's. He accused the Russian government of fostering anti-Semitism and acting upon it; he saw current attacks on the reputation of the great Jewish writer Isaak Babel, dead in a Stalinist camp, as not exclusively anti-Semitic but an attack on the human spirit itself, as represented by the freedom of art, the complication of art and by the peculiar loyalty of art to reality.

Though hating to speak in public I found myself doing so, incensed by constant claims that religion was necessary for morality. I had never believed this. A religious man can be as cruel, fanatic, destructive as anyone else. The danger was not that of Jew, or Gentile, religion or atheism, but that of indifference, less to dramatic and sensational enormities but to the long grind of everyday prejudice and unkindness. Atheists and agnostics had joined in, or even founded, vast humanitarian projects: the League of Nations, the World Health Organization, the United Nations, UNESCO.

I have known fine, even outstanding Jews, Christians, Moslems, who have retreated into the isolation of cell, study, or their own souls. I have known those who have not. The great Norwegian explorer, diplomat, sportsman, humanitarian, Nansen, set a moral example to the world; agnostic, he was hailed as the conscience of Europe. He too would have agreed that the heresy today is in standing aloof from actual people, and that, for high-sounding reasons, you can do appalling things, for a time, then, indifferent to their effects, continue in power as if nothing had happened. It was known two thousand years ago, in Greek Tragedy, when Odysseus, acting vindictively, bloodily, declares: 'We will be honest men . . . later on.'

It is not ignorance that now imperils us, but lack of imagination; not so much active persecution, common though that is, but passive refusal to act, to speak out, a danger which, like disease and corruption, is creeping, insidious, ultimately fatal. I remind you, as I have reminded myself, that we are talking in a city where a great writer, Emile Zola, in a situation not entirely dissimilar, risked name and fortune by taking a risk. He dared speak out.

Writers much younger than myself were, from the sixties onwards, marshalling themselves: Kingsley Amis, Colin Wilson, John Braine, John Wain, John Osborne. The Angry Young Men quackery, however, passed me by; I was not young, I was slow to anger. In time I was goaded into boasting to myself that, through Jan van Leyden in *The Friends of God*, I had been my own Angry Young Man – raging against the truth permitted to the herd, the truths reserved for the élite; against fur-coated slum landlords, hypocritical lawgivers, masters of eloquent deception:

> I understand your fears, I can understand everything, and in rebelling against those like you, fat in your own lies, scalded by your own thefts, is not my hope of salvation for I have saved myself without help from you. But, in throwing back your plunder at your filthy teeth, remains hope for those that come after and by whom I shall be remembered until the sea swallows up the last of your great bellies and plundered meadows.

Journalists spun around the young a vulgar notoriety which detracted from their useful talents. The Angry Young Men of my childhood had been Hitler and Mussolini – 'Hit and Mus' sang the wits of Unity Theatre – Michael Collins and Eamon de Valera, von Salomon and Ernst Juenger, Mosley, Huey Long, James Maxton. Unable to extract myself from springtime, formative influences, I could not compare our Angry Young Men with anything very considerable.

John Braine I had met in the full flush of acclaim for *Room at the Top*, usually in his cups; I thought him hectoring, abusive, over-confident. Years later he was changed, with a failed marriage, critical disregard, financial worries and ill health, and was sadly grateful to be joined at a table, offered a drink, reminded of his excellent book on Priestley. His old rivals and associates were now comfortably enthroned in the academic posts, official honours, media slots they had once ridiculed. His own attempt to sell his manuscripts in an effort towards security failed, the reserve not reached. Sunk in ominous gentleness, he seemed too dispirited to show anger or self-pity. I began liking him, but soon he was dead.

Not so Arnold Wesker, small, bright-eyed, combative without rancour, urgent to report from his experiences in lower-depths London and Paris. 'I want to teach.' Gorky and Shaw would have agreed more strenuously than Coward and Rattigan. Kenneth Tynan wrote of Wesker in 1967: 'He came closer than any other English dramatist to demonstrate that socialist realism was not a dogmatic formula but a uniquely powerful means of conveying some theatrical emotion.' It was a socialism that, like my ex-wife's, I could feel and understand; not that of Fabian committees handing down blueprints and granting benefits to the deserving poor but something full-blooded, generous, with the emotional and practical cohesion of a mining community, often coarse and vulgar but part of that surging existence I had found in Dickens, Gogol, Wells, in Pritchett, in Dostoevsky, in Gorky, in Jaurès.

Tynan was someone I seldom met, though kept constantly aware of him as yet another self-advertising personality, also a serious champion not only of the raw, aggressive, demotic Theatre of Anger but against insular tastes, advocating Pirandello, Genet, Beckett, Brecht, Tennessee Williams, Arthur Miller.

Complementary, yet irreconcilable, Miller and Williams have produced the most powerful body of dramatic prose in modern English. They write with equal impetuosity, Williams about the violets, Miller about the rocks. The vegetable reinforces the mineral; and the animal, a dramatic element feared or ignored in the English theatre triumphantly reinforces both.

(Here he overlooked David Storey, who, as novelist and dramatist, neither feared nor ignored the animal.)

Tynan enjoyed comparing Miller to Shaw, as sharing 'a belief in progress towards an unattainable summit; an awareness of the outer world of intolerance and curable wretchedness, of politics and bad housing, prejudice and superstition'.

Seldom fooled for very long by the ring of bright phrases, save perhaps by his own, Tynan provoked much personal opposition, as he always intended. 'Rouse tempers,' he had advised himself, 'goad and lacerate.' He succeeded with apparent ease. In old age Kingsley Amis blamed him for 'the general, trendy, left-wing, show-biz – Zen Buddhism, pot-smoking, bull-fight cult – American "happening" subculture'. Ralph Glasser – shrewd, caustic, working class – despised affluent dinner-jacketed socialist academics with their country homes and, like Victor Gollancz, exclusive air-raid shelters, who patronized working-class novices. He remembered Tynan at Oxford, one of the fashionably half-baked, with his 'stick-like thinness, the purple suit flapping on him as on a skeleton, his sunken cheeks and lips stretched tight over jutting teeth', a careerist, a flaunting opportunist. Yet, Glasser conceded, in *Gorbals Boy at Oxford* (1988), he was more than display and calculation:

> Hidden away in his unique mixture of banality, tinsel brilliance and showmanship, was a mysterious, startling insight, revealing itself in the telling comment, apt as an arresting newspaper caption but containing much more – at its best a profound personal concern, shyly displayed and then hidden once again beneath the raucous and superficial

At Oxford Tynan charged an entrance fee at his party for Gertrude Lawrence, for which I know no undergraduate precedent.

Of my *The Game in the Ground* Tynan told me: 'Talent is insufficient, it has limits. Only genius . . .', his tone more wistful than dismissive. I disliked him yet regretted, as I had with so many others, that I had not spent a few leisurely hours alone with him. Was he, I wondered, ever alone? He gathered about him, like income, even more stories than Paul

Potts, remembered with discrimination by his widow Kathleen in her 1987 biography. She recalled his dislike of the rattle of loose change in his pocket, so that he would throw pennies into the street, like the Gentleman in Shaw's *Village Wooing*, always throwing away halfpennies.

He seemed a gloss on Byron's belief that the great object in life is sensation; in the lineage of the English, French and Irish Dandy. Of Milan Cathedral he judged, 'Too pizzicato. No calm passages. Every spire and gargoyle shrieks "Look at me." Secure cathedrals say, "I'm looking at you."' His bull-fight rhapsodies I thought pretentious, lacking genuine scholarship in pagan ritual and Iberian tradition, though with the intellectual's hankering for crafted violence seen from the front stalls, unmindful of Henry James's belief that a bull-fight would, to a certain extent, bear looking at but not thinking about. As one who had experienced blood and death in the Blitz, I was repelled by wanton violence. I could not envisage a Tynan adventuring in Korea, the Congo, Northern Ireland. And I read without admiration William Burroughs's letter to Jack Kerouac: 'Been seeing a lot of bull-fights. Good kicks. Going to a cock-fight this evening. I like my spectacle brutal, bloody and degrading.' Hitler's diagnosis is less archaic than I had once supposed.

> Cruelty impresses. People want a good scare. They want something to make them afraid, someone to whom they can submit with a shudder. Have you noticed, after a brawl at a meeting, that the ones who get beaten up are the first to apply for Party membership? What is this rot you talk about violence and how shocked you are about torture? The masses want that. They need something to dread.

Kathleen Tynan thought her husband self-invented and brilliant. As a schoolboy collecting mocking-birds, grey rats, dragonflies, enjoying cricket, he had reflected: 'Eccentricity, like all forms of surreal art, must come from within, and must be creatively egoistic.' Afterwards, he liked 'cigarette-holders, large signet-rings and Eton crops'. His flamboyance – his father's surname was Peacock – did not diminish. At his first wedding he wore a green carnation; he lunched with Alec Guinness in billiard-table green; he wore pink feathers on a burgundy-coloured dinner-jacket. That remark of his about talent and genius was probably significant. His inability to produce a work of art, despite lively essays and perceptions, needed compensation, by making a minor masterpiece of himself, a self-drama sustained by power as newspaper critic and in the National Theatre.

Dying too young, Tynan had added his mite to the tragi-comedy of British life. Maria Riva describes how her mother, Marlene Dietrich, arriving at the Dorchester suite, discovered behind a couch a white worm – Tynan – whom she had heard was England's leading dramatist. A drink soothed his nervousness, his talk initiated a lasting friendship.

'Tynan wrote many things about my mother, always brilliant, always to the point, but nothing as true as my favourite: "She has sex without gender." In my opinion, the best analysis of Dietrich's professional enigma.'

Usually, I felt more at ease with those slightly older than myself with whom I shared references already becoming esoteric or anachronistic: Zeppelin, the Somme, the Depression, the New Deal, Amritsar, Sun-Yat-Sen. The young despised my lack of status; the old did not notice.

Most were good company. Not least was an actor whom I met at the Arts Theatre Club, styling himself in French fashion only as 'André', though baptized Mark Custard. He had charm without much professional success, but while his achievements were few they were singular. He caused discussion on a radio chat show: when asked to name the second most interesting personality in the New Testament he replied 'Jesus'. He won a fair-sized bet by wagering that, as Polonius, he would successfully insert into his speech to Laertes a *Daily Telegraph* editorial. Always believing that to separate personal foibles from his career would 'betray life', he once disguised himself as a parson and, invited to preach at a Herefordshire church, delivered a sermon in honour of Zeus, which aroused no comment whatsoever. For a friend's party he guaranteed to produce a Maori head, a Maid of Honour and a live jay. His forecast that he would die of Aids was faulty: he was killed crossing the road to avoid hurting the feelings of a virulent drama critic by cutting him.

George Mikes, another link with historical Europe, was a small, alert, merry-eyed Hungarian journalist, famed for his *How to Be an Alien*. He knew an author who regularly and unsuccessfully canvassed on behalf of various candidates for the Nobel Prize for Literature, not from unstinted regard for their work but to obstruct Theodore Dreiser. Eventually, George wrote:

> On learning that canvassing in one's own interest was possible, I asked an Academician friend point-blank, 'What about me?' He raised his eyebrows and asked me why I wanted it. 'Well,' I replied, 'it is good propaganda, it helps one to get along, and I should also like the money, provided it was tax-free.' He might vote for me – my friend added on further reflection – and there were two elderly members who would vote for absolutely anyone. 'That made three.' He felt, however that the remaining fifteen 'would take time'.

Certainly that year, for some reason, they preferred Hemingway.

A.J. Ayer I knew better. His quick, darting head, alert eyes, brisk manner reminded me of a bird. Our relationship, until Vanessa Ayer's death, was only agreeable tittle-tattle about sport, mutual friends, movies, childhood. In gossip, he was easily superior.

'Freddie, is there anyone you haven't met?'

'Yes. Queen Mary, Adenauer, yes – and Wallis Windsor.'

Late in life he wrote a book on Voltaire, in whom he had no interest, professed not to have read, to secure a large advance he had suggested only as a joke.

'Freddie, I suppose you've read some Voltaire?'

'Nothing.'

'But now, you'll read a bit of him.'

'Of course not.'

Inasmuch as I understood his philosophy, it suited me: the dependence of ideas on scientific evidence and rigorous scrutiny of language, to deflate the pompous rhetoric so often masquerading as truth. He was accused, like Socrates, of corrupting youth by moral nihilism. I was indignant. A sexual freebooter, he had yet seemed to me a philosophic puritan, wrecker only of stale beliefs, large but unproven, usually unprovable, metaphysics. His morality was not of sexual conformism but of indignation against racialism, racketeering, false prophets, windy demagogues. Indeed at times I found him too moralistic; we disagreed over the morality of the Nuremburg Trials, he insisting that they were a most dangerous legal precedent and that the presence of Russian judges vitiated the last remnants of justice towards the accused. I welcomed de Gaulle's return to power in 1958 but again on moral grounds, Freddie disagreed, maintaining that, to settle one problem – Algeria – even by just means would ultimately create an even larger problem for France, too often attracted by charismatic authoritarianism, leading to disaster.

Freddie's atheism was not negative or cynical but a positive injunction to replace God by using analytical intelligence and realizing one's potential, ceaselessly testing facts, speculating further, challenging one's own discoveries, admitting error gracefully, returning to the attack. I remember the alacrity with which, to refute some solecism I had committed, he showed me Karl Jaspers's 1950 essay 'Marx and Freud'.

> The style of Marx's writings is not that of the investigator, he does not quote examples or adduce facts which run counter to his own theory but only those which clearly support or confirm that which he considers the ultimate truth. The entire approach is that of vindication of something asserted as perfect truth with the conviction not of the scientist but of the believer.

This could have been written by Ayer himself, eager to pounce on a weak link in a chain of reasoning to rip away verbiage in a manner I always found friendly, entertaining, if caustic. He loved soccer and cricket, chess and bridge. He favoured Jane Austen and Dickens but was a tireless reader of detective stories and thrillers – he had worked briefly for Secret Intelligence. He enjoyed Belloc's *Cautionary Tales* and could quote from his *The Servile State* and, of British thinkers, most admired Hume and Russell. He was much drawn to Hollywood musicals and prewar songs. I too was helpless against the insidious, gossamer authority of tunes.

The only lecture of his I ever attended, his farewell to London University in 1959, had theatrical, almost balletic *élan*. He had transformed the London Philosophy Department from a stagnant backwater to international standing. The first holder of the Chair, the Revd Hoppus, held it for thirty-seven years without, Ayer commented, contributing to his subject anything of the slightest importance.

Admitting a ready disinclination to forego attention to himself, he liked telling the Queen of Greece anecdote, which appears in his autobiography. It began at an Athens Conference of the International Institute of Philosophy, where later he and his colleagues were 'entertained, if not feasted' by Queen Frederika, a German amateurishly concerned with determinism. This continued in London during her visit with King Paul where, driving through the streets with Queen Elizabeth and the Duke of Edinburgh, the party was hooted at by crowds for her alleged pro-Nazi sympathies, the Duke scrutinizing the dissidents 'like Sherlock Holmes in an ugly mood'.

Later, in Claridge's, Queen Frederika lunched Freddie, along with the Greek poet-diplomat George Seferis, Graham Greene, Frederick Ashton, Harold Nicolson and the scientist Lord Adrian. Freddie had anticipated a brief but animated discussion after lunch between these assorted notables, to which the Queen would listen like a courteous pupil, interrupting only to call for another bottle. However, as he wrote in 1984 in *More of My Life*:

> We were made to sit in a large semicircle converging on Queen Frederika, who proceeded to lecture us for nearly two hours on the philosophy of science. Graham Greene made an intervention, which was brushed aside, I made several ineffective attempts to argue in what Harold Nicolson described in his diary as my 'exquisite manner'. I have always suspected that this phrase was ironical. Afterwards I remonstrated with Lord Adrian for his remaining silent on a subject in which he was much better qualified to speak than I, but he merely thanked me for protecting him.

I had to keep my head with Freddie. He was fluent in Spanish, French, German, could refute me by citing leading thinkers in a dozen traditions; his weakness, I felt, was not only his knowledge but his understanding of history. He overlooked, or dismissed, the contributions of poets, dramatists, novelists to historical understanding, speaking, at least to me, as if people of the past, though in curious attire and with picturesque language, thought much as we do. I disagreed, urging that to our ancestors, a colour, a bird, a footprint, a name, number or star, meant something very different; they had very different meanings to us both. 'You . . . historical relativism . . . nonsense,' he would say, his smile, swift, affectionate, forgiving but not convincing me. I could imagine him nodding tolerant assent to 'nothing is so dumb as a god's mouth', but deploring or feigning incomprehension, when accosted by 'Who, if I cried, would hear me among the angelic orders?' until snappily replying 'No one' or amending this to 'H.H. Price' with polished self-acclaim at producing a name of which I knew nothing.

Otherwise his thought was ready-made for me. Despite constant references by others to his relationship to the thought of Wittgenstein, Frege, the Vienna Circle, he seemed to me very much in the common-sense, logical, humanist British empirical tradition not only of Russell but also of Roger Bacon and Francis Bacon, Occam, Hume and, in a less refined way, of Orwell and much of Wells. I write, however, from a very vulnerable position: I have never read *Language, Truth and Logic*, let alone *The Foundations of Empirical Knowledge*. References to Ryle, Austin, Price, Carnap and, at that time, Popper meant nothing to me. Our conversations are the only foundations of my view of him. These, after some thirty years of amiable but lightweight consequence, deepened after Vanessa's death, though his own followed all too quickly. As friends, we had obstacles to overcome: my own apathy towards philosophy and admiration for his wit, incisive rejoinders and intellectual scholarship; his indifference to my novels and contempt for my thought. My lingering religious interest he thought childish, with an agility always outpacing me. An indefinable mutual affection bonded us not, I fear, very closely but with a future, had not death, like Mr Berkeley Pell, said a few quiet words.

Ayer's death occasioned considerable, sometimes hostile evaluation. Many younger friends and students recalled his wit, stimulus, kindness.

Others indicted him for vanity, prejudices, his assumption that, as if by natural right, he was always in the chair. Roger Scruton thought him a liberal socialist busybody, helping to destroy the grammar schools while sending his own son to Eton. He labelled Freddie as a hater of wisdom, and 'It would have needed only a page of George Eliot, a line of Shakespeare, to discredit Ayer's conception of the moral life.' Freddie did not hate wisdom but he disliked capital letters, woolly metaphysics and pomposity masquerading as wisdom and ignoring ascertainable facts. Earlier, though he had actively served in the liberation of France, given lifelong support to ethnic and sexual minorities, he had been ludicrously assailed not only for élitist but fascist tendencies from those whose contributions to civilization were farcical. Freddie honoured friendship, the values of truth, social justice, traditional good manners and sportsmanship. His departure impoverished me; a few inscribed books, some letters in that tiny handwriting, these memories. I can add witness to some hours of happiness. It was a luncheon given by Dorothy and V.S. Pritchett: Freddie and Vanessa were there, with Derwent and Yolanta May, the historian John Clive, Margot Walmsley, and, I think, Janet Adam Smith. A splendid meal – salmon trout, imaginative salads, carefully chosen wines – accompanying rare currents of friendship, the goodness of earthly life a lasting gleam across a dark and distressing winter.

Freddie I liked; Vanessa I loved. She was beautiful, vivacious, liable to mock, infinitely considerate. A confession that I had not read some book, some journal, would be instantly followed by the arrival of the one, a subscription to the other. Returning home late at night, sometimes despondent, I would find some gift on the doorstep, always anonymous but it could only have been from her. At a party of mine she was always at the centre of a laughing, disputing circle, but I was horrified to learn from another friend that she had only a month to live. My farewell letter, very short, taxed me more than any of my books. Her reply was typical: she gave, accurately, the date of her passing, asked me to read at her memorial service a lesson, which she had already chosen, and ended by a generous reference to a book of mine which she was very much hoping she would have time to finish.

The reading has always puzzled me, Psalm 6; it seemed to me unlike her, surely containing a code known only to her intimates, certainly to Freddie, hunched, broken, inert. It is a dirge of guilt, lamentation, grief, ending on a note of vengeful hope:

> All my enemies shall be confounded and dismayed;
> they shall turn away in sudden confusion.

At parties, I still watch the door in almost superstitious expectation of certain vanished friends suddenly appearing. They are a little late but on their way: Shirley, Margot, Stephen, V.S.P., Freddie and Vanessa, like the roses in Rilke's poem, enriching the room where they have come to settle for a while.

8

CONCLUSIONS

There is something singularly attractive about men who retained throughout life, the manners, the texture of being, the habits and style of a civilized and refined milieu. Such men exercise a peculiar kind of personal freedom which combines spontaneity with distinction. Their minds see large and generous horizons, and, above all, reveal a unique intellectual gaiety of a kind that aristocratic education tends to produce. At the same time, they are intellectually on the side of everything that is new, progressive, rebellious, young, untried, of that which is about to come into being, of the open sea whether or not there is a land that lies beyond. To this type belong those intermediate figures, like Mirabeau, Charles James Fox, Franklin Roosevelt, who live near the frontier that divides old from new, between the *douceur de la vie* which is about to pass and the tantalizing new age that they themselves do so much to bring into being.

– Isaiah Berlin

B Y 1999 I had published some forty-five books, contributed to a dozen more, a small output compared to that of the Distant Planets. A plodder, never a trim flyer, I am nagged by convictions, not of torpor but of unadventurousness, indeed laziness, especially since learning from Fenton Bresler in 1984 that the young Simenon wrote eighty pages a day, ninety-two words a minute – once, in a single month, producing five novels, each of 70,000 words. This made me seem paralysed.

Already the very intensity of the creative prose would cause his stomach muscles to knit together like steel and he would be forced to break off the writing and run to the wash-basin to vomit. Even in his later, assured years of success, this distressing symptom would constantly recur.

Though unenviable, this was formidable, and I remembered marriage with renewed guilt. My wife would return from her office exhausted, scarcely breathing. 'Dreadful day. All this work!' Gradually recovering, she would glance at my writing table, over-tidy, over-clean. 'Well, Peter, how was your day?'

'Ah, I've been hard at it too. I went to a movie – to pick up the Mediterranean background, of course. Bardot . . . yes, well . . . then I went to a café with Rudi and Emanuel . . . to watch how people actually move between tables. And I overheard something very useful . . .'

Grounds for divorce, I imagine, in eleven American states.

Against life I have no complaints. I survived the Blitz, managed a few rescues: I have avoided torture, exile, jail; critical contempt for my first book preserved me from conceit and illusions. Much of my work has been published, though no book sold above 3,000 copies, and I often wondered why publishers persisted, though without risking cross-examining them. In hospitable households I find books of mine, the marker inexorably stuck on page three. Other writers tell me that, after publication, they hire a secretary to deal with their mail. For me, an occasional letter arrives out of the horizon, with such information that blackbirds lack orange beaks.

I was once dining at Flanagan's, Baker Street, with Freddie Ayer shortly after Vanessa's death. He was, understandably, dispirited.

'You too must often feel, by now, that it's not been worth it. I at least have had the vulgarity of success, money and fame which mean very little, but mean rather more if you've not got it.' He recovered slightly, looked about for the wine waiter, 'But for you . . . you write books which nobody reads, you wouldn't call yourself a conversationalist . . .'

I expected him to compare me to Evelyn Waugh's unpleasant 'Mr Beaver', invited only at the last moment, in emergency. Then, on the waiter's departure, I rallied. 'Yes. All the same, though . . . I like to feel that nobody else could have written my *Parsifal* novel . . .'

Freddie considered this, presumably with his verification through sense-data principle on hand. Then his customary incisiveness returned: 'Would you say that anyone else would want to?' Whenever tempted towards complacency, I remember this, also Mrs Osborne and Auberon Waugh cavorting in critical ragtime like a music-hall turn.

Michael Hamburger, a friend of much longer standing, titled his

1973 autobiography *A Mug's Game*, referring to his vocation as poet, translator, authority on German and European literature. I do not think so of my own, which has granted me sterling friendships, a few interesting commissions, some sly forays in those suggestive back-alleys and small tributaries, a prolonged process of self-discovery. There is marvellous freedom in writing and reading and living entirely as I wish.

Apathy, moreover, has not yet set in like pack-ice. Baudelaire sometimes felt himself a child in a theatre, eager for the show, hating the curtain; after the curtain rose he was still waiting. I too am still waiting, though much of the show I have enjoyed.

Entering old age, I found – through the accident of a publisher taking seriously a chance remark – new stimulus in compiling five anthologies. Part of me always wanted to teach, to share excitements, to push doors a little wider. Anthologies were pavilions with many doors through which to probe, hesitate, explore or hastily withdraw. Some rooms were stacked with the discarded, which yet secreted the poignant or mysterious, some were virtually empty, mere atmosphere but with something valuable though still concealed. Some had shadowy, enticing nooks, others were crudely glaring, crammed with good taste, the fashionable, the correct. The best had windows opening to vistas still obscure, perhaps forbidden but irresistible. *Tell our stories.*

The anthologies at school had been worthy but ponderous and predictable, and I usually looked in vain for depths of dream and twilight, the barely seen and somewhat sinister fairy-tale range of de la Mare's *Come Hither* poetry anthology and the unexpected, mischievous and inconsequential.

> Julius Caesar Pompey Green
> Wore a jacket of velveteen.

In arranging my own, I enjoyed, I suppose, the satisfaction that the curator of an art exhibition feels in deploying his choices in unifying relationships, balancing, uncovering analogies, with here a dissonance, there a coincidence not at first sight discernible. From those trailing notebooks I could swiftly extract much that had unfrozen my imagination. 'Another's heart is a dark forest' (Turgenev). 'For she is tall as a lance, and as fresh as an April morning' (Cervantes). 'A lady who looked as if she had swallowed the east wind' (Wodehouse). 'I loved thee once, Atthis, long ago' (Sappho). By no means forgetting Laurence Eusden, Poet Laureate, commenting on his employer, George II:

> Hail, Mighty Monarch, whom desert alone
> Would, without birthright, raise up to the Throne!
> Thy virtues shine particularly nice,
> Ungloomed with a confinity to Vice.

In my anthology of the French Revolution I attempted to develop characters – Mirabeau, Louis XVI, Napoleon – from their own utterances. Robespierre's clammy smile, horror of physical contact, his tinted glasses and fastidious externals, could unscramble into early oppression by loneliness, poetic and humane yearnings, premature responsibilities, his repulsive chilliness concealing a tumult of compassion, impatience, indignation, hope. I rejoiced when chancing upon the Goncourts' description of Robespierre and Jacques-Louis David as two icy geniuses in a volcano and traced a graph between youthful idealism and the Terror, between Robespierre's belief in 'that tender, impetuous and irresistible passion, torment and delight of magnanimous souls', and Hébert's fearful 'To be safe we must kill everyone.' It was exciting to unearth from a long-extinct Paris journal: 'The guillotine's first victim was Nicholas-Jacques Pelletier. The people were by no means satisfied. They had seen nothing. It was all over too swiftly. They went away disappointed.'

I sought the bizarre and curious together with the momentous, heartfelt and significant and discovered memorability in the trivial. I was glad of a letter from Tom Paine to Thomas Jefferson:

> A man came into my room, dressed in the Parisian uniform of a Captain, and with a good address. He told me that two young men, Englishmen, were arrested and detained in the guard house, and that the Section had sent him to ask me if I knew them, in which case they would be liberated.

This matter being settled between us, he talked to me about the Revolution, and something about (my) *Rights of Man*, which he had read in English; and at parting, offered me, in a polite and civil manner, his services. And who do you think the man was who offered me his services? It was no other than the public executioner, Sanson, who guillotined the King, and all who were guillotined in Paris, and who lived in the same street with me.

Not important, yet not easily forgotten.

Work, a declaration of independence, never finishes; if it threatens to, it is best not to admit it, then work harder, not toadying to the past or shirking the future. Survival tactics entail periodic self-scrutiny, needs for renewal, and, approaching eighty, a fresh start is essential. Fresh vision through well-rooted slants. I have known too many writers who succumbed to Toynbee's 'idealization of a dead self, the nemesis of creativity', in which a society – Sparta, Athens, Venice – perfects a style but clings to it too long, and this, with failure to transcend it, hardens into a prison. Some friends, with early successes, strove not to go forward but to repeat them; visions became clichés, ideas crumbled into platitudes. In her old age I met Stella Gibbons, whom I had thought long dead. That she had been a poet was forgotten; of her many stories and novels only *Cold Comfort Farm* was remembered, but this had given her immense fame and had added phrases to the language. She told me, with gentle humour and without rancour, that now she could get none of her work accepted. Fashions, methods, language, editors, publishers had changed in ways foreign to her temperament, style, material. She still had much to say but could no longer find ways to say it acceptable to new audiences. I admired her fortitude, was sobered by her tale and was glad to see her number of devoted friends, amongst them John Braine.

I must now, though with gratitude, escape Woolf, Broch, Proust, Mann, as earlier I had Feuchtwanger, Mitchison, Duggan, Jack Lindsay, earlier still Dumas and Orczy. Indeed I must require no models. This is never easy. My friend Professor Valerie Minogue's championship of Nathalie Sarraute's novels encouraged me to study them, and indeed they forced me to reconsider fiction, use imaginative muscles rusted or hitherto undiscovered. The verve of much younger writers has periodically helped recharge me: Robert Nye, Julia O'Faolain, Iain Sinclair, Lawrence Norfolk, Robert Lipscombe, Derek Beaven, all help erase the pull of my own novels, of which I am not ashamed but which are, or should be, part of the dead self. The moribund excites only repetition. In their mythic reality these writers crush barriers between past and present, myth and fantasy, seen and unseen, I and It. Few much-vaunted British novelists are producing work of the imaginative force of Michel Tournier's *The Erl King*.

For me, the strength of sentences, of language, outbids the necessity for radical experiment in overall design and method. *Doctor Zhivago, The Aunt's Story, Humbolt's Gift* have originality in line but do not dazzle by architectural freakishness. I admire Faulkner but have no wish to emulate the confusions, however true to life, of *The Sound and the Fury*.

I must explore science more energetically to reinforce my evidence, toughen my metaphors. Predominant is the necessity for vigilance, awareness of the pressures of a glance, a silence; to observe more thoroughly some figure isolated within a crowded party, a loud dinner, jungaloid train, existing in slower time, in different society, with the stillness of a scholar reading and the silence when a hangman enters.

I retain my habit of writing two books simultaneously. In my Estonian contemporary novel I develop my hankering for the Baltic north, its light, ports, forests, its thousand years struggle against Teutons and Russians. For the second, I still have only a title, *1870: The Terrible Year*, and the opening sentence: 'The god Hermes was seated at a table in rue Castelnau, at the Café Charles Moreau.' There is still only the merest glimmer, but from this a novel may emerge, boundless, free, the true masterpiece which all novels are, until they are actually written.

Angus Wilson told a wry story. He was at work in his garden. A child passed.

'Look, Mummy . . . there's an old man writing.'

'Yes, darling. It does them so much good.'

For years I usually fancied myself the youngest at any gathering. Now, with most contemporaries dead or reclusive, and younger friends turning aside, though not myself actually on crutches, I assume I am by far the oldest, resigned to offers to hold my arm to cross three feet of floor or being tapped like a barometer by those anxious to stack me away. In defensive tactic I tend to exaggerate my age rather boastfully so that 'When I was young . . .' suggests an epoch Minoan or biblical. 'Yes. I remember the *Titanic*. As she sailed past, I couldn't help thinking . . .'

I remind myself that years are inventions of priests. The year 2000 AD is already producing high-flying proposals and verbiage without scarcely a mention of what it, on unsteady evidence, actually commemorates. Real birthdays, I have to insist, are days of rebirth; vital initiations, moments of glory. First day at school, losing virginity, certain deaths and encounters, acceptance of the first book, birth of the first child. With luck I shall reach not eighty but fifteen.

At whatever age life can still sparkle with catalysts and oddities. A neighbour spent his savings on printing a tome, with an appendix of 600 pages of statistics, disproving the fingerprint method of detection. I envied a young peer, whose obituary in 1997 mentioned him being accosted in Central Park by armed muggers demanding his money. Asked afterwards what he had done, he replied, in the tradition of Sir Percy and Psmith, of Brummell, Disraeli, Ken Tynan, 'I simply ignored them, of course.' An entire thesis is suggested by that 'of course'.

Like the experts, I am not acute in observing the larger world and was astonished by the collapse of the Berlin Wall and USSR, the liberation of the Baltic states and Eastern Europe. My notebooks were filled not with prophecies but with minor selections from the passing scene, to be used as best I could. Eisenhower, accused of starving to death a million German prisoners of war in 1945; Britain reviled for, at Stalin's request, destroying exquisite Dresden, very loudly by those foremost in reverencing 'Uncle Joe'. The Sinn Feiner, Gerry Adams, condemned Britain's opposition to Hitler as 'an imperialist adventure', though Ireland's benefits from a Nazi victory remain obscure. The European Court of Human Rights, once hailed by Churchill as protection against dictatorship, ordered Britain in 1996 to compensate relations of Irish terrorists killed in Gibraltar, when primed to commit indiscriminate slaughter. A Moscow newspaper claimed that, under Brezhnev, happiness had increased by 94 per cent. Maoist China condemned Beethoven's Sonata for Piano and Orchestra as expressing the filthy nature of the bourgeoisie.

Throughout, I have feared the irrational, meaningless violence, the delights of mindlessness. Two boys with high IQs planted a home-made bomb under a Midlands town hall; John Lennon's murderer explained that by killing him he would acquire his victim's fame; Lucien Léger slaughtered a child in order to be mentioned in newspapers. The great revolutions attracted such types, often concealed by momentous upheavals, by the massive and global.

Youthful cynicism was buttressed by elderly men coding the Alamogardo plutonium bomb tests 'Trinity'. Bob Dylan was cheered in five continents for his wisdom: 'Politics is bullshit. The only thing that's real is inside you. Your feelings.' My pupils were enthralled by Mao, Castro, Guevara, as heroes battling for humanity in exotic terrain and against the odds. Under the Russo-American Balance of Terror neutrality seemed cowardly evasion. Execution and massacre were irrelevant, the new heroes were of the martyr breed saluted by Lenin and Gorky, and indeed Himmler, as accepting the tasks of history to kill some in order to save others. My own scepticism entailed some unpopularity amongst the young, which sometimes hurt, but I could only follow my temperament. I wanted carved on my gravestone 'He looked for evidence.' Hating committees, I preferred to sit on a few, rather than howl in mass demonstrations.

There were other dissidents, often less publicized, of whom I was becoming aware, whose adventures and struggles in South Africa, Eastern Europe, Asia, the southern states of the USA, Latin America would make an encouraging book to accompany those of youthful volunteers working in medicine, agriculture, education, charity amongst remote peoples. I did begin a history of 'Peaceful Change', appropriating the title from a book I had read at school, but the material overwhelmed me in its bulk, I lost stamina and left it for others who would manage it better. Details and personalities have remained. There was Frederic Born, of the International Red Cross, saviour of scores of Hungarian Jews; countless unglamorized men and women risking their lives to rescue, succour, salvage; amongst them was Father Jerzy Popieluszko, Polish priest, defender of the shipworkers' union Solidarity against the one-party Russian-held state. He defied martial law and his own Church hierarchy, until, aged thirty-seven, he was kidnapped, beaten, drowned. Like Wallenberg and hundreds more, he followed Karl Kraus, who maintained that if he had to choose the lesser of two evils he would reject both.

Ageing gives me temptations to adopt grosser neutrality, cultivate solitude like a garden, wallow in the past. I watch old movies, reliving wondrous, youthful afternoons. Thus I see them in treble dimension, for the stars throw long shadows before them: Leslie Howard, Hollywood's 'Scarlet Pimpernel', shot down by Nazis into the Bay of Biscay, together with my own friend, Wilfrid Israel, a real-life Scarlet Pimpernel who had saved thousands in Hitler's Germany; Ramon Navarro, murdered; Carole Lombard, in all her cool beauty, crashing from the sky; Vivien Leigh, barely sane; George Sanders, elegant and imperturbable, chatting in some hotel to Louis le Brocquy, the artist, until mounting the stairs towards suicide; that last, cruel sight of David Niven, gaunt, raddled, dying; Judy Garland, whom I saw in London before her suicide. She was to perform, she was very late; we awaited that voice bounding off all walls like a surreal squash ball – at last she appeared, drunk or drugged, forgetting her songs, swearing at the audience who had loved her but now shouted and booed.

A perfect writer, Whitman asserted, would make words sing, dance, copulate, bear children, weep, bleed, rage, stab, fire cannons, steer ships, sack cities, charge with cavalry or infantry, do anything that men and women with natural powers can do. Kipling said much the same.

I have always loved language, its gifts of precision, nuance, fluidity, and early learnt from ballads, with their stark simplicity, so powerful that a later, morally pretentious age feared them. Thomas Wilde's *A Little Book for Little Children* (1617) carried a health warning: 'When thou canst read, read no Ballads or Foolish Books, but a Bible and *The Plain Man's Pathway to Heaven*.' Children should also read 'Other Treatises on Death and Hell and Judgement'. Avoiding these I was grateful to Kipling and Auden for continuing the ambiguous simplicity and fateful enchantments of fairy-tale and ballad, continued by my contemporary, Charles Causley, who must have been a godsend to several generations of children.

> Hurry to harbour, Sailor,
> Fetch the parson by noon,
> Or the fox will lie with your lover
> Under the mask of the moon.
>
> Down by the springy river,
> Down by the shrieking locks,
> Watching love die like a doctor
> Is the patient Mr Fox.
>
> Your coat, Mr Fox, is of satin,
> Your wallet as gold as a harp,
> The gloves on your delicate fingers
> Hide your nails so sharp.

Language is threatened not only by electronic codes but from within, by slovenly journalists, political correctness, professional jargon. I remember Cyril Connolly writing in 1944:

> The English language is like a broad river on whose banks a few patient anglers are sitting, while higher up, the stream is being polluted by a string of barges tipping out the muck of Fleet Street and the BBC . . . Words today are like the shells and ropes of seaweed, which a child brings home glistening from the beach and which in an hour lose their lustre.

I remember Lionel Trilling puzzled to learn from students that by teaching Jane Austen he was assisting the Vietnamese war. Language remains the most subtle and versatile means of communication; when language dies, imagination withers, or so I had always thought. This, however, was disputed even by those whose fortunes depended on it. 'Language is, quite simply, fascistic,' Roland Barthes maintained, 'every form of classification is oppressive.' André Breton had already declared that language was a bourgeois strait-jacket inimical to pure creativity and freedom. Daily I read stuff that would have momentarily stifled Cyril Connolly: 'Massification of the Individual'; 'Manifestation of optical and acoustical razzamatazz'; 'He made a bold conjecture about the relation between the classification of vector bundles by stable isomorphism and their classification by stable homotopic equivalence of the association sphere-bundles.' I cannot believe that many poets hasten to learn from Julia Kristeva: 'The notion of constructibility which implies the axiom of choice associated with all we have put together for the poetic language explains the impossibility of establishing a contradiction in the space of the language of poetry.'

The poet Joseph Brodsky declared that evil, especially political evil, is always a bad stylist. I remembered this when reading in an Irish book that Lord Mountbatten's death was 'the result of an explosion in his fishing boat'. Accurate yet untruthful. 'Why not name the thing?' Cobbett had once thundered. He would rage at media show-offs, with their tiny vocabularies, unremitting clichés and pseudo-democratic patois, the overall bromide which evokes nostalgia for the seventeenth-century Thomas Fuller: 'Anger is one of the Sinews of the Soul: he that lacks it hath a marred mind.' Salman Rushdie has written that democracy can flourish only in turbulence.

I have visited schools, sometimes on an Arts Council project, where the logic and clarity of a Shaw, Russell, Orwell were dismissed by teachers as devices to obstruct demotic speech, thus élitist and reactionary. I have heard classics derided as conspiracies to mislead youth politically and sexually.

All this makes me remember with more respect my own teachers and even, perhaps particularly, the Gentleman Rankers. When I read: 'It is needful to centralize the production of educated juveniles', I feared the elimination of a certain school tone – wayward, amateurish, humorous, tolerant, philistine but not grossly so and allowing for solitude, minorities, the independent. Thomas Mann once wrote that education is a matter of atmosphere. H.G. Wells thought education the building up of imagination. Mass schooling has been compulsory since 1870, but a recent survey of 900 pupils, aged eight to sixteen, found less than 50 per cent able to find London on a map, over one-third ignorant of the location of Scotland and, in Scotland, only 38 per cent able to place Edinburgh; 42 per cent could find Germany, 18 per cent knew that the Acropolis was Greek, 19 per cent were ignorant of the Pyramids and the Statue of Liberty. Such polls suggest that what should happen often does not. A Chinese poll in 1990 admitted that despite, or because of, years of Marxist indoctrination 68 per cent chiefly desired 'riches'; the same seems applicable to post-Soviet Russia.

Educational poverty is scarcely surprising, though I was startled to read an admission by Lady Mary Warnock, much respected for her work for the 1978 *Warnock Report* on children with special needs:

> To condemn comprehensive schools on purely academic grounds seems 'élitist', and no accusation is more damning. Both Left and Right, for different reasons, are compelled to avoid such a charge, for the penalty of élitism is that all one's arguments are automatically disregarded. It was fear of the charge of élitism that led many members of the House of Lords, including myself, to sit in cowardly silence when the title of University was bestowed on all polytechnics indiscriminately.

I am élitist in that I prefer Glenlivet in finely spun glass to instant coffee in airport cardboard, a Schubert *Lied* to 'The Song the Old Cow Died Of' and would have no shame in demonstrating to some academic demagogue that a 'value judgement' can be risked between *King Lear* and *Getting Gertie's Garter*.

Further timidity was displayed by an *Oxford English Dictionary* issued for Russia in 1985. An editor explained that his dictionaries were adjusted for different markets, so that 'Capitalism' was here defined as 'an economic and social system based on private ownership of the means of production operated for private profit and on the exploitation of man by man'. Presumably this has now been revised.

Like most of us I resent humbug. I spend no half-hours comforting those in cardboard boxes, but I do keep open a spare room. I have no inclination to be spokesman for those who have never heard of me.

Objections to euphemism and correctness is not to plead for a linguistic freeze-up. Vernacular can be lively and suggestive, like prison slang: 'fist full' (five-year sentence), 'bird drag' (mental stagnation from prolonged imprisonment), 'gobbling behind hedges' (grievous bodily harm). For better, for worse. I have watched speech infected by standardization. A sentence by D.H. Lawrence, unexceptional in my boyhood, now requires an encyclopedia. 'Orion marching above: how the dog-star Sirius looks at one, looks at one! He is the hound of heaven, green, glamorous and fierce.' Days, months, skies are saddled with the antique, often incomprehensible, perhaps, perhaps not, due for renaming, with the thrills of a writer primed before a page still blank.

In my novel *Lancelot* King Arthur's sceptical associate muses that anyone can name a sea, but who can discover a sea and find a name corresponding to his explorations? 'I myself,' Lancelot adds, 'am intelligent enough to ask such questions but not to answer them.'

The tired earth her riches sheds. I do not much bother about age, only fitfully consider the future and have not yet discovered convincing evidence for historical inevitability. The outcomes of the Battles of Britain and Stalingrad, which saved theorists from extinction, conformed to no obvious laws. For myself I find in 'What shall I do today?' more freedom, of choice, of being, than anything guaranteed by bills or declarations of rights, free constitutions or people power. At present I tend to believe that we possess less free will than we like to believe but that it is expedient and more enjoyable to behave as if we have plenty, in the spirit of Shaw's query when Tolstoy rebuked his frivolity: 'Suppose the world were one of God's jokes, would you work any the less to make it a good joke instead of a bad one?'

E.M. Forster once said that death destroys a man but that the idea of death saves him. Another view, of course, was delivered by a republican on the death of Charles I: 'God's work, done in God's way.' Meanwhile, God or no God, I am content with a garden and tiny cottage, though I would enjoy having a long gallery and a stream and am mindful of a Rothschild dictum that no garden, however humble, should contain less than two and a half acres of rough woodland.

I still admire the resilience, the individuality, of those in the Isaiah Berlin paragraph quoted above and the defiance of the tenth-century German nun Hrotswitha, Europe's first woman dramatist, 'a writer of considerable merit but great coarseness' who, when her works were rebuked for indecency, merely replied, 'Nevertheless, they please me.'

Reviewing, in 1997, *On History* by the eighty-year-old Marxist historian Eric Hobsbawm, I was moved and encouraged by his concluding words:

> Much of my life, most of my conscious life, was devoted to a hope which has been plainly disappointed, and to a cause which has plainly failed: the communism initiated by the October Revolution. But there is nothing which can sharpen the historian's mind like defeat.

In a longish life, what have I myself achieved? Worldly success? No. Contentment? No. Happiness? On the whole, yes. My next novel rests on the favour of the god Hermes, and I may yet reach my fifteenth birthday.

INDEX OF NAMES

Abse, Dannie, 88
Acton, Lord, 132
Adorno, T.W., 87
Alcott, Louisa May, 13, 29
Alfred the Great, 30, 61
Amis, Kingsley, 91, 109, 162, 164
Amis, Martin, 118
'André' (Mark Custard), 166
Annan, Noël, 93
Athill, Diana, 77
Attlee, Clement, 116, 140
Auden, W.H., 9, 15, 38, 42, 66, 101,
    103, 108, 116, 121, 130
Aurelius, Marcus, 67
Austen, Jane, 59, 116, 119, 168
Ayer, A.J., 104, 133, 167–72, 174
Ayer, Vanessa, 171–2

Babel, Isaak, 88, 89, 116, 161
Baldwin, Stanley, 41
Barthes, Roland, 183
Baudelaire, Charles, 175
Bayley, John, 17, 104
Beaven, Derek, 178
Beckett, Samuel, 138, 140, 163

Bedford, Sybille, 91
Belloc, Hilaire, 168
Bely, Andrei, 30–1
Berlin, Isaiah, 48, 49, 98, 99, 173
Bevan, Aneurin, 55, 145–6
Blanch, Lesley, 29
Blok, Alexander, 71
Blunt, Wilfrid, 25
Boothby, Robert, 47
Borges, Jorge Luis, 73
Born, Frederic, 180
Bowen, Elizabeth, 127
Boyars, Arthur, 88
Braine, John, 162
Brecht, Bertold, 53, 88, 163
Breton, André, 183
Broch, Hermann, 16, 125
Brodsky, Joseph, 183
Brophy, Brigid, 53
Bryant, Arthur, 78
Bryce, Lord, 64, 101
Buchan, John, 13, 20, 91
Buckingham, George, 1st Duke, 60
Buckingham George, 2nd Duke, 66,
    134

Burkhardt, Jacob, 62
Burgess, Anthony, 108–14, 129
Burroughs, William, 136, 165

Canetti, Elias, 87, 88–9
Carey, John, 114
Causley, Charles, 108, 182
Cavafy, Constantine, 106, 125
Cervantes, Miguel, 117, 176
Chapman, Guy, 118
Chekhov, Anton, 50, 71, 72, 73, 135
Chesterton, G.K., 20, 59, 61
Church, Richard, 117–18
Churchill, Winston, 27, 45–9, 53, 63, 140, 179
Cobbett, William, 183
Cocteau, Jean, 11, 157
Comfort, Alex, 48, 78
Connolly, Cyril, 70, 138, 182
Conquest, Robert, 144
Cosman, Milein, 88
Crippen, H.H., 154
Cromwell, Oliver, 65

Dalton, Hugh, 144
David, Jacques Louis, 63, 176
Davidson, J.C.C., 47
de Chirico, Giorgio, 45, 130
de Gaulle, Charles, 48, 168
de la Mare, Walter, 18, 175
Dickens, Charles, 59, 69, 125, 168
Dietrich, Marlene, 166
Dimitrov, Georgi, 40–1
Djilas, Milovan, 48, 145
Dostoevsky, F.M., 83, 86, 116, 125, 163
Drabble, Margaret, 115, 118, 119

Edel, Leon, 48
Ehrenburg, Ilya, 160
Eliot, T.S., 23, 54, 100, 102, 117, 152
Elton, G.R., 63
Eugénie, Empress of France, 11
Eusden, Laurence, 176

Fairbanks, Douglas, 21
Fermor, Patrick Leigh, 30
Feuchtwanger, Lion, 31–2, 39, 85, 89, 125
Fischer, Ernst, 41
Flaubert, Gustav, 74
Fogarty, Elsie, 37
Forster, E.M., 100, 116, 126, 128, 129–30, 185
Fowles, John, 116
Fraenkel, Michael, 88
Franklin, Edward, 82
Franz Josef, Prince of Lichtenstein, 67
Fraser-Smith, S.W., 24
Frederika, Queen of Greece, 169
Fuller, J.F.C., 47

Gabor, Zsa Zsa, 37
Galen, Bishop Clemens von, 147
Gandhi, Mahatma, 26, 83
Gardiner, A.G., 46
Garland, Judy, 181
Garret, Tony, 119
George V, 21

Gibbons, Stella, 177
Gibson, Robin, 63
Gide, André, 64, 73, 88
Gielgud, John, 97–8
Ginsberg, Allen, 104
Gladstone, W.E., 66
Glasser, Ralph, 164
Goering, Hermann, 36, 40–1, 68
Golding, William, 85, 109
Gorky, Maxim, 71–3, 125, 163, 180
Grahame, Kenneth, 67
Greene, Graham, 20, 109, 117, 127, 150, 169
Gunther, John, 62

Haile Selassie, Emperor, 40
Halifax, Lord, 13
Hamburger, Michael, 174–5
Hardy, Thomas, 51
Hart, Basil Liddell, 47
Hartley, L.P., 127
Hayman, Ronald, 31, 97, 135
Hearne, J.T., 62
Heller, Erich, 91
Hemingway, Ernest, 167
Henriques, Fernando, 156
Hensher, Philip, 128–9
Himmelfarb, Gertrude, 91
Hitler, Adolf, 47–8, 50, 65, 156, 162, 165
Hobsbawm, Eric, 143, 146, 186
Holroyd, Michael, 47, 49
Howard, Leslie, 181
Hrotswitha of Gandersheim, 186
Hugo, Victor, 31, 64

Huizinga, Johannes, 130–1
Huxley, Aldous, 39, 52, 102, 105

Isherwood, Christopher, 53
Israel, Wilfrid, 95, 181

Jackson, J. Hampden, 78
James, Henry, 46, 54, 85, 92, 165
Jaspers, Karl, 168
Jay, Douglas, 145
Jesse, F. Tennyson, 155
Jesus, 38, 74, 79–80, 81–2
Johnson, B.S., 114
Jones, Ernest, 19
Joos, Kurt, 130
Joseph, Keith, 91
Joyce, James, 23, 31, 51, 73, 102, 110–11, 129
Juenger, Ernst, 68, 100, 162
Jung, Carl Gustav, 39

Kassil, Lev, 98
Keenan, Barney, 111–12
Keller, Hans, 88
Kenyon, John, 93
Keynes, John Maynard, 65
King, Francis, 108, 109
Kipling, Rudyard, 18, 23, 115, 118, 120, 135, 181, 182
Koestler, Arthur, 10, 58
Kraus, Karl, 88, 181

Laing, R.D., 19
Laski, Marghanita, 119–20
Lawrence, D.H., 54, 79, 108, 185

Lawrence, T.E., 12, 50
Leavis, F.R., 34, 129
Leavis, Q.D., 34, 127
Lehmann, John, 99–100, 102
le Neve, Ethel, 155
Lessing, Doris, 120–1, 140
Letwin, Oliver, 91
Letwin, Shirley Robin, 91–3, 172
Letwin, William, 91
Levy, Paul, 128
Lewis, P. Wyndham, 39, 74, 127
Lipscombe, Robert, 178
Litvinoff, Emanuel, 88, 160, 174
Lively, Penelope, 114
Lo, Kenneth, 26
Lorca, Federico García, 134
Lucretius, 37–8
Luxemburg, Rosa, 54, 63

Macaulay, Lord, 62
Mack Smith, Denis, 40
Magee, Bryan, 53, 55, 92
Malraux, André, 39, 138
Mankowitz, Wolf, 160
Mann, Heinrich, 31, 32
Mann, Thomas, 31, 38, 130, 132, 135, 183
Mao, Chairman, 10, 143, 180
Marx, Karl, 23, 168
Mary, Queen, 21, 167
Masefield, John, 9–10, 61–2
Mason, A.E.W., 20
Maugham, W. Somerset, 69, 77, 95, 148
Melnikov, F., 137

Meyerbeer, Giacomo, 33
Mikes, George, 166–7
Miller, Arthur, 145, 163, 164
Minogue, Kenneth, 145
Minogue, Valerie, 177
Molotov, V.M., 43
Montgomery, Field-Marshal Bernard, 50
Morozov, Pavlick, 14–15
Mosley, Oswald, 109, 139, 162
Muir, Edwin, 43, 69
Murdoch, Iris, 17–18, 88, 127
Murry, John Middleton, 78–9
Mussolini, Benito, 12, 39–40, 55, 162
Myers, L.H., 34–5

Nabokov, Vladimir, 31
Namier, L.B., 99–100
Nansen, Fridjof, 161
Napoleon III, 11, 65
Nassauer, Rudolf, 85–90, 121, 137–8, 148, 174
Neumann, Alfred, 31, 39, 125, 132
Nicolson, Benedict, 127, 133, 135–6
Nicolson, Harold, 126, 169
Nicolson, Nigel, 127, 135–6
Norfolk, Lawrence, 178
Nye, Robert, 178

Oakeshott, Michael, 91, 92
O'Faolain, Julia, 178
Orczy, Baroness, 19–20
Orwell, George, 26, 35, 78, 170
Osborne, John, 34, 92, 162
Owen, Peter, 88, 126

Paine, Tom, 176–7
Pasternak, Boris, 30
Peake, Mervyn, 42
Pearson, Hesketh, 49–50
Peter, Gabor, 144
Petrarch, 65
Pilenko, Elizabeth, 101
Pinter, Harold, 145
Popieluszko, Jerzy, 181
Potter, Dennis, 12
Potts, Paul, 122–4
Pound, Ezra, 23, 27, 50, 54, 71, 91,
   102, 105, 140
Powell, Anthony, 100, 109, 115, 117,
   127
Priestley, J.B., 43, 56, 74, 75, 103, 116,
   163
Pritchett, V.S., 33, 49, 56–8, 64, 71, 76,
   114, 127, 128, 171, 172
Prokosch, Frederick, 73
Pushkin, Alexander, 27

Quiller-Couch, Arthur, 107

Raymond, Ernest, 155
Raine, Kathleen, 52
Read, Herbert, 46–7
Redgrave, Michael, 43
Rilke, Rainer Maria, 39, 81, 85, 130,
   134, 143, 151, 157, 170, 172
Rimbaud, Arthur, 116, 130, 134
Riva, Maria, 166
Robespierre, Maximilien, 176
Rochester, Lord, 134
Rogers, P.H. 'Val', 101

Roosevelt, Franklin D., 35, 45, 48, 50,
   63
Ross, Alan, 24–5, 75
Rowse, A.L., 107–8
Rubens, Bernice, 85
Rushdie, Salman, 183
Russell, Bertrand, 54–5, 65, 161, 168

Salomon, Ernst von, 68, 162
Sanders, George, 37, 181
Sansom, William, 91
Santayana, George, 148
Sappho, 176
Sarraute, Nathalie, 114, 177
Sartre, Jean Paul, 51, 53
Savage, D.S., 78, 128
Scholl, Hans, 147–8
Scholl, Sophie, 147–8
Scholl, Inge, 147–8
Schweitzer, Albert, 51, 79, 80, 101,
   161
Schwitters, Kurt, 130
Scott, Beatrice, 88
Scott, Walter, 80
Scruton, Roger, 170
Shaw, George Bernard, 12, 33, 36, 43,
   49–53, 56, 67, 164, 165, 185
Simenon, Georges, 134, 173
Simpson, F.A., 68
Sinclair, Iain, 178
Sitwell, Osbert, 78
Solomon (pianist), 11
Souter, Ian, 152
Spark, Muriel, 123, 160
Spender, Stephen, 97, 101–7, 128, 172

Stalin, Josef, 43, 48, 50, 62, 73, 89
Stanford, Derek, 87, 123
Steiner, George, 86
Stendahl, Krister, 93–5
Storey, David, 163
Strachey, Lytton, 47
Symons, Julian, 57

Taylor, A.J.P., 12, 48, 51, 53, 136, 145
Tennyson, Alfred, 27
Thomas, Edward, 59
Tippett, Michael, 110
Tiptoft (Lord Worcester), 64
Tolkien, J.R.R., 121–2
Tolstoy, Leo, 32, 37, 71, 72–3, 185
Tolstoy, Nikolai, 67
Tournier, Michel, 178
Toynbee, Arnold, 53, 91–2, 98–9, 177
Toynbee, Philip, 66, 133
Trevelyan, G.M., 63, 107
Trevelyan, Raleigh, 108
Trilling, Lionel, 161, 182
Turgenev, Ivan, 176
Turnbull, William, 88
Tynan, Kathleen, 164–5
Tynan, Kenneth, 163–6, 179

Uglow, Euan, 88

van Leyden, Jan, 33–4, 162
Vansittart family, 11–12
Vansittart, 'Jackie' (author's wife), 27, 80, 120, 133, 135–6, 140, 163, 173–4
Vansittart, Mignon Thérèse (author's mother), 10–11, 13

Waddell, Helen, 28
Wallenburg, Raoul, 101, 181
Walmsley, Margot, 95, 171
Walpole, Hugh, 69, 115
Warnock, Mary, 184
Wasserman, Jacob, 28–9, 39, 146
Waugh, Auberon, 118, 174
Waugh, Evelyn, 46, 53, 118, 174
Wayne, John, 29
Webb, Beatrice, 91, 144
Weisel, Elie, 159
Wells, H.G., 20, 23, 43, 45, 47, 50, 53–4, 56, 65, 84, 85, 101, 103, 125, 137, 170, 183
Werfel, Franz, 31, 69, 88
Wesker, Arnold, 163
Wesley, Charles, 14
West, Rebecca, 51, 52, 128
Whitman, Walt, 123–4, 181
Wilde, Oscar, 45, 133
Williams, Tennessee, 163
Wilson, Angus, 88, 109, 114–19, 178
Wilson, Colin, 53, 88, 162
Wilson, Francesca, 91
Wodehouse, P.G., 34, 81, 135, 137, 176
Woolf, Leonard, 41, 100–1
Woolf, Virginia, 54, 102, 106, 125–30
Worsthorne, Peregrine, 92, 93, 153–4

Yeats, W.B., 105, 141
Yourcenar, Marguérite, 133

Zweig, Stefan, 31, 88